HONDURAS
state for sale

Latin America
Bureau

First published in Great Britain in 1985 by **Latin America Bureau** (Research and Action) Limited, 1 Amwell Street, London EC1R 1UL.

Published with the assistance of The World Council of Churches. The views expressed, however, are those of the authors.

British Library Cataloguing in Publication Data

Lapper, Richard
   Honduras: state for sale
   1. Honduras—History
   I. Title
   972.83 F1506
   ISBN 0-906156-23-8

Written by Richard Lapper and James Painter
Maps by Michael Green © Latin America Bureau
Cover illustration © Kevin Kallaugher
Cover design by Chris Hudson
Typeset, printed and bound by Russell Press, Nottingham
Trade distribution in UK by Third World Publications,
   151 Stratford Road, Birmingham B11 1RD
Distribution in USA by Monthly Review Foundation

Contents

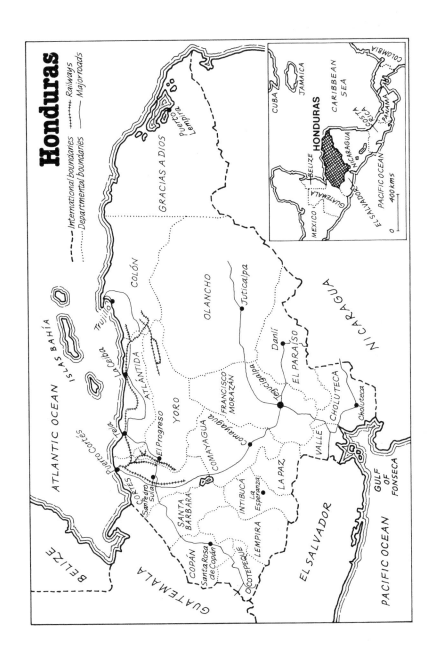

iv

1 Honduras in Brief

Country and People

Area		112,088 sq km
Population	Total	4.3 million (1984)
	Growth	3.6% (1975-80)
	Urban	23% (1960)
		37% (1982)
Principal Cities	Tegucigalpa	533,600
	San Pedro Sula	397,900 (1982)

The People	Origins	Mixed 90%; Amerindian 7%; African 2%	
	Principal indigenous groups	Carib	(15,000)
		Opatoros	(15,000)
		Sumo	(15,000)
		Jicaque	(10,000)
		Morenos	(7,000)

Language		Spanish
Religion		97% nominally Roman Catholic
Health	Life expectancy	59 years (1981)
	Infant mortality	95 per 1,000 live births (1975-80)
	Population per doctor	3,124 (1979)
	Hospital beds	1.4 per 1,000 people (1979)

1

| *Education* | Literacy | 60% (1980). 22% of those enrolled in primary education proceed to secondary education. Percentages of relevant age group for attendance in secondary and higher education are 21% and 8% respectively. |

The Economy

GDP	Total	1983	US$1,301 million
	Per capita	1970	US$313
		1984	US$314
	Per capita growth	1981	−2.3%
		1982	−5.1%
		1983	−3.8%
		1984	−0.6%

| *Labour Force* | | Agriculture 57%; Manufacturing 15%; Construction 4% (1980) |

Inflation	1979	18.9%
	1980	15.0%
	1981	9.2%
	1982	9.4%
	1983	10.2%
	1984	6.9% (March to March)

Real Wages	1979	11.5%
	1980	8.3%
	1981	5.1%
	1982	−1.0%
	1983	−8.2%
	1984	−4.6%

Trade	Exports	1981	US$784 million
		1982	US$677 million
		1983	US$695 million
		1984	US$740 million
	Imports	1981	US$899 million
		1982	US$681 million
		1983	US$761 million
		1984	US$750 million

Major Exports	Bananas 35%; Coffee 22%; Wood 7%; Meat 5%; Shrimps and Lobsters 4%; Silver 2% (1982)

Major Trading Partners

Exports to:	US 54%; Japan 6%; Guatemala 4%
Imports from:	US 48%; Venezuela 10%; Japan 6%; Guatemala 6% (1983)

Foreign Debt (total)		
	1978	US$971 million
	1981	US$1,708 million
	1982	US$1,800 million
	1983	US$2,079 million
	1984	US$2,250 million
Debt per capita	1984	US$523
Debt service as ratio of total exports	1977	7.2%
	1981	14.5%
	1982	22.4%
	1983	17.7%
	1984	19.0%

Sources: CEPAL; *Comercio Exterior;* Inter-American Development Bank; the International Institute for Strategic Studies; *South* magazine; World Bank.

Chronology

1502	Christopher Columbus lands on the northern coast of Honduras.
1821	Honduras wins independence from Spain as a member of the Central American Federation.
1839	The Federation breaks up and Honduras becomes an independent republic.
1876-1883	Marco Aurelio Soto and Ramón Rosa establish Honduras' first Liberal regime.
1899	The first banana concession is granted to the Vaccaro brothers (later to become Standard Fruit).

3

1907	The US banana merchant, Sam Zemurray, forms the Cuyamel Fruit Company.
1912	The Trujillo Railroad Company wins a contract to build a railway, marking the beginning of United Fruit's involvement in Honduras.
1916	The first recorded strike takes place on Cuyamel's banana plantations.
1929	United Fruit buy Cuyamel from Zemurray for US$32 million.
1932-1948	Sixteen-year dictatorship of General Tiburcio Carías Andino.
1948	The Nationalist Juan Manuel Gálvez takes over as president.
1952	The Francisco Morazán military college is set up.
1954	A military treaty is signed between Honduras and the US. 50,000 workers in the banana belt go on strike. Julio Lozano Díaz is appointed to the presidency.
1956	Lozano exiles Liberal leaders and crushes armed rebellion. The armed forces seize power for the first time.
1957	The Liberal leader Ramón Villeda Morales wins elections.
1961	Honduras joins the Central American Common Market.
1962	First agrarian reform is introduced.
1963	Colonel López Arellano leads military coup against Villeda.
1965	López is confirmed as president after standing as Nationalist candidate in elections. The peasant leader, Lorenzo Zelaya, is killed and his guerrilla column destroyed.
1969	The 'football war' with El Salvador breaks out and lasts for 100 hours.
1971	The Nationalist Ramón Ernesto Cruz wins presidential elections.
1972	'National Unity' government falls apart. Seven peasants are killed at La Talanquera near Juticalpa. López Arellano directs second coup in November. Second agrarian reform.

1975	Third agrarian reform. López resigns after the 'Bananagate scandal' and General Juan Melgar Castro takes over as president. The army and local landowners kill 15 peasant demonstrators, including two priests, at Los Horcones.
1977	The government intervenes against the peasant co-operative at Las Isletas.
1978	Melgar Castro is replaced by a three-man junta led by General Policarpo Paz García.
1979	Following the overthrow of the Nicaraguan president, Anastasio Somoza, in July, the Carter administration strengthens its relations with Honduras.
1980	The Liberals win Constituent Assembly elections, but the interim presidency is handed over to General Paz García.
1981	Liberal Party candidate, Roberto Suazo Córdova, beats the National Party candidate Ricardo Zuñiga by over 100,000 votes in the November presidential elections. John Dimitri Negroponte takes over as US ambassador. The US National Security Council approves US$19 million for covert operations against Nicaragua.
1982	*January:* President Suazo Córdova is inaugurated. First session of an 82-member Congress takes place with 44 Liberals, 34 Nationalists, three PINU and one Christian Democrat. Colonel Alvarez is approved as head of the armed forces. The government introduces economic austerity measures.
	February: The Reagan administration pledges a 50 per cent increase in military aid to Honduras. Four clandestine cemeteries are discovered.
	April: Cinchonero guerrillas hijack an airliner, but release their hostages with their demands unmet. The government passes decree law No.33, making strikes and land occupations 'subversive acts'. Alvarez is promoted to general.
	June: The Honduran army takes part in joint operations against the FMLN with the Salvadorean army. Sixty student and trade union leaders are arrested. Alvarez and Suazo visit Washington to negotiate a major increase in military aid.
	July: Honduran guerrillas blow up an electricity

generating plant in Tegucigalpa, and counterinsurgency units storm a guerrilla safe house, also in the capital.

August: The Honduran armed forces are put on full alert · after border clashes with Nicaragua. 30,000 teachers go on strike.

September: Cinchonero guerrillas hold San Pedro Sula businessmen in the city's chamber of commerce building, but leave without securing their demands.

November: Newsweek reveals that Negroponte is in overall control of *contra* operations against Nicaragua.

1983 *January:* The right-wing pressure group APROH is founded, with Alvarez as its president.

February: 'Big Pine I' joint US-Honduran military exercises begin, involving 1,600 US and 4,000 Honduran troops.

May: Alvarez signs a secret agreement in Washington to set up the CREM regional training centre at Puerto Castilla.

June: First US trainers and Salvadorean troops arrive at the CREM. In Mexico City, five Honduran political-military organisations announce a unity pact.

August: Biggest ever military exercises, 'Big Pine II', begin, involving 5,500 US troops.

September: A guerrilla column of the PRTC is destroyed by the army in Olancho. Father James Guadalupe Carney, a US priest who had joined the guerrillas, is among those killed.

1984 *January:* Alvarez presents a new constitution for the armed forces.

March: Power workers' leader, Rolando Vindel, is kidnapped. Alvarez is overthrown by younger officers and forced into exile. Four other generals are forced to resign.

April: Air force chief General Walter López takes over command of the armed forces. 'Grenadier I' manoeuvres start on the Honduran-Salvadorean border and include Salvadorean troops. The naval exercise 'Ocean Venture' also begins.

May: 60,000 demonstrators in Tegucigalpa and 40,000 in San Pedro Sula protest against the US presence. The new military leadership begins efforts to re-negotiate the 1954 military treaty and the CREM.

June: A general strike against the new taxes, planned primarily by the CTH, is called off at the last minute.

August: In a cabinet reshuffle, Carlos Flores Facussé loses his job as minister to the president.

September: The tax increases stopped by the threat of a general strike in June are finally introduced. Power workers' union STENEE launches a strike to demand reappearance of Vindel.

October: The FBI breaks up a coup plot in Miami, involving the former Honduran chief of staff, Colonel Bueso Rosa.

November: APROH is disbanded.

December: The army publishes its report into human rights violations, blaming 'left- and right-wing non-Hondurans' for the disappearances.

1985 *January:* Steadman Fagoth, leader of the MISURA *contras,* is expelled. The National Congress of Rural Workers (CNTC) is formed.

February: 'Big Pine III' exercises begin.

March: 'Constitutional crisis' breaks out.

April: 'Universal Trek '85' troop manoeuvres begin.

May: 'Constitutional crisis' ends after pressure from the US, the army and trade unions. Suazo and López travel to Washington to seek more aid and an amendment to the 1954 treaty.

June: The CREM is closed. 'Cabañas '85' military exercises begin.

August: The Honduran army enters the Colomoncagua refugee camp, kills two Salvadorean refugees, wounds fifty and takes away ten others as prisoners.

September: Border incident between Nicaragua and Honduras is reported to have left one Honduran soldier dead and two Nicaraguan helicopters badly damaged.

POLITICAL PARTIES

Partido Liberal (PL) — Liberal Party

The governing party from 1957-63 and from 1981 until the present. The origins of Liberalism lie in the nineteenth-century anti-Spanish and anti-clerical reform movement. Historically, the party's principal support base has been divided between a conservative wing of large landowners, small farmers and the rural middle class and a more radical current based in Tegucigalpa and San Pedro Sula. The conservatives won control of the party in the 1960s under Modesto Rodas Alvarado, lost it between 1967 and 1974, but have been dominant ever since. The *rodista* tendency backed Suazo Córdova's presidential campaign in 1981 and dominated the 44 Liberal seats in Congress. The more progressive tendency, ALIPO, a group of business interests based mainly in San Pedro Sula, remained marginalised within the party. Since 1981, *rodismo* and ALIPO have both divided. *Rodismo* split into three: (1) the *suazocordovistas,* like Oscar Mejía Arellano and Carlos Flores Facussé, who control the party apparatus and favour closer links with the army, (2) a faction loyal to Efraín Bú Girón, the president of Congress, and (3) the *azconistas,* who support José Azcona del Hoyo, a centre-right technocrat and former public works minister to Suazo. ALIPO split into two in 1984: (1) MOLIDER, a small social democrat group based in Tegucigalpa and led by Carlos Roberto and Jorge Arturo Reina, and (2) the original San Pedro Sula-based group who have banking, trading and real estate interests, and control one of the country's leading newspapers, *Tiempo.*

Partido Nacional (PN) — National Party

Although there were attempts to create a National Party from the 1890s onwards, the Nationalists emerged as a coherent group only in the early 1920s as a split from the Liberals, and remained the only other main party until the mid-1960s. Originally deriving their support from large landed interests, particularly in backward departments like Intibucá and Lempira, the party is historically more conservative than the Liberals, and is often labelled 'the civilian wing of the armed forces'. In the wake of the crushing electoral defeat of 1981, the party divided into several factions, the most important of which are the supporters of Ricardo Zuñiga, who fought the 1981 election; the Movement for Unity and Change (MUC) which favours close links with the military and is headed by Juan Pablo Urrutia; and two other tendencies led by old-style *caudillos* Mario Rivera López and Rafael Leonardo Callejas, who are in favour of keeping a distance from the army.

Partido de Innovación y Unidad (PINU) — Innovation and Unity Party

A small centrist party with support among urban professionals and some labour movement leaders. Formed in 1969 after the 'football war' by Miguel Andonie Fernández, PINU holds three seats in congress. Julín Méndez of ANACH has been a PINU congressman since the 1981 elections and is the only peasant leader in the legislative. PINU's leader is Enrique Aguilar Cerrato.

Partido Demócrata Cristiano de Honduras (PDCH) — Christian Democrat Party

Initially a peasant-student movement in the early 1960s, the PDCH was formed in 1968, and is the most progressive of any Central American Christian Democratic party. The party's base is in the two trade union federations linked to it, the CGT and the UNC. Hampered by the opposition of the Liberals and Nationalists to its legal registration, the PDCH won only one seat in the 1981 elections. The sole deputy, Efraín Díaz Arrivillaga, is the most outspoken critic of Liberal/military policies within Congress. Díaz represents the party's left wing, while trade union leaders Marcial Caballero and Felicito Avila are supporters of the party's right wing. Internationally affiliated to the Christian Democrat World Union. Its leader is Hernán Corrales Padilla.

Parties not holding seats in Congress (prior to 1985 elections):

Partido Comunista de Honduras (PCH) — Communist Party

Formed in 1954, the PCH is the pro-Moscow section of the Communist Party, and the oldest and strongest of Honduras' left-wing parties. It was internally divided in the 1960s and 1970s over whether to work through the existing unions or to form independent federations. The United Federation of Trade Unions (FUTH) was set up in 1981 under PCH domination. The party joined the 1981 electoral alliance, the Patriotic Front (FPH), with the PCH-ML and PASOH, which failed to win any seats.

Partido Comunista de Honduras — Marxista-Leninista (PCH-ML) — Communist Party (Marxist-Leninist)

Formed by PCH dissidents in 1967 who supported China in the Sino-Soviet split, the PCH-ML's main strength is in the teachers' unions, COLPROSUMAH and COPEMH.

Partido Socialista de Honduras (PASOH) — Socialist Party

Formed by Christian Democrat dissidents following the 1975 Los Horcones massacre, the party is a strong supporter of a confrontational approach to rural problems. It has links with the

PRTC, whose destruction in 1983 included a number of PASOH leaders.

There are four small guerrilla organisations:

Movimiento Popular de Liberación 'Cinchoneros' (MPL) — Popular Liberation Movement

Named after a nineteenth-century peasant leader, the MPL was formed by students at the National Autonomous University (UNAH) after the Nicaraguan revolution. They came to prominence in 1982 when they hijacked an airliner and held a number of businessmen hostage in the San Pedro Sula chamber of commerce.

Fuerzas Populares Revolucionarias 'Lorenzo Zelaya' (FPR) — Popular Revolutionary Forces

Named after a peasant leader in the 1960s, FPR also emerged from students at UNAH. The FPR is committed to a strategy of 'prolonged popular war'.

Frente Morazanista de Liberación Nacional de Honduras (FMLNH) — Morazanist Liberation Front

The FMLNH is the armed wing of the PCH-ML.

Partido Revolucionario de los Trabajadores Centroamericanos — Sección de Honduras (PRTC-H) — Revolutionary Party of Central American Workers

Led by José María Reyes Matta, a group of around 100 members of the PRTC crossed from Nicaragua into Olancho in July 1983. By mid-September, up to 40 guerrillas, allegedly including the leader and a US priest, Father James Guadalupe Carney, were killed and the group virtually eliminated.

In June 1983, the PCH, FMLH, Cinchoneros, FPR and PRTC-H formed an alliance, the National Unitary Direction (DNU), but it has remained dormant.

TRADE UNIONS

According to official figures, there were 290 unions in 1979 with around 142,000 affiliates, out of a total labour force of 1,210,500. The trade unions themselves claim much higher membership numbers. There are three main trade union organisations:

10

Confederación de Trabajadores de Honduras (CTH) — Honduran Confederation of Workers

Founded in 1964, the CTH unifies the three pro-US and pro-ORIT federations formed in the late 1950s and early 1960s, the Federation of Workers' Unions of the North (FESITRANH), the Central Federation of Honduran Free Trade Unions (FECESITLIH) and the National Association of Peasants (ANACH). The CTH unites 72 unions and over 100,000 workers. Of the 43 member unions of FESITRANH, the banana workers' unions SITRATERCO (United Fruit) and SUTRASFCO (Standard Fruit) are the largest. CTH leaders are closely linked to the American Federation of Labor (AFL-CIO) and many have been trained on courses run by the American Institute for Free Labor Development (AIFLD). In general, the CTH is strongly anti-communist and the least combative of the federations. The secretary of the CTH is Andrés Víctor Artiles.

Central General de Trabajadores (CGT) — General Congress of Workers

The CGT is a Christian Democrat federation formed in 1970 by the Authentic Trade Union Federation (FASH), the Federation of Southern Unions (FSS) and the National Union of Peasants (UNC). According to union figures, it has 78 affiliated unions and over 125,000 members. Affiliated unions include textile, bank and construction workers, and slum-dwellers' associations. The CGT is aligned with the right wing of the Christian Democrat party and is affiliated to the Latin American Confederation of Workers (CLAT) and the World Confederation of Labour (WCL). Its funds come principally from West German and Venezuelan Christian Democrat sources. CGT's secretary-general is Felicito Avila.

Federación Unitaria de Trabajadores de Honduras (FUTH) — United Federation of Workers

Formed in 1981 by the PCH and PCH-ML, FUTH has 30 affiliated unions, of which the water workers (SITRASANAA) and the electricity workers (STENEE) are the most important. Internationally affiliated to the pro-Moscow Permanent Congress of Trade Union Unity of Latin American Workers (CPUSTAL). Its president is Napoleón Acevedo.

11

PEASANT UNIONS

There are four main peasant associations:

Asociación Nacional de Campesinos Hondureños (ANACH) — National Association of Honduran Peasants

Formed in 1962, ANACH is a member of the CTH and the largest of the peasant unions. According to government figures it has 23,000 members; according to ANACH, 80,000 members and 638 branches. Its major strength lies in the north, with a smaller presence in Olancho, Comayagua and the west and south of the country. The most pro-US and least combative of the peasant unions, ANACH usually seeks technical assistance and prefers a non-confrontational approach to rural conflicts. Its president is Julín Méndez, who is also a deputy in Congress for PINU.

Unión Nacional de Campesinos (UNC) — National Union of Peasants

UNC grew out of ACASCH (the Social-Christian Peasant Association) in the 1960s to be formally constituted in 1970. It is a member of the CGT and closely linked to the Christian Democrat movement. The second largest of the unions, it has 20,000 members according to government figures, 75,000 according to the UNC figures. Its main strength is in Olancho, Copán, Choluteca, Comayagua and Cortés. The UNC is divided between a right-wing tendency led by Marcial Caballero (who is secretary-general), now in control, and a more leftist tendency headed by Marcial Euceda.

Federación de Cooperativas de la Reforma Agraria (FECORAH) — Federation of Agrarian Reform Cooperatives

Created as part of the agrarian reform in 1970, FECORAH unites 57 agricultural cooperatives. According to government figures, it has 6,000 members. In general, it is pro-government and conservative. Its president is Efraín Díaz Galeas.

Central Nacional de Trabajadores del Campo (CNTC) — National Congress of Rural Workers

Formed in 1985, the CNTC is an attempt by independent and left-wing unions to build a united movement. It includes the National Authentic Union of Honduran Peasants (UNCAH), a 1977 split from UNC and ANACH with around 10,000 members; the National Union of Popular Cooperatives (UNACOOPH), formed in 1977 with around 2,300 members; the Unitary Federation of Peasant Cooperatives

(FUNCACH); the National Front of Independent Honduran Peasants (FRENACAINH), a 1977 split from ANACH; and an organisation linking associate peasant enterprises in the north (EACH). The CNTC on the whole represents what was left of the previous unity organisation, the National Unity Front of Honduran Peasants (FUNACAMH), formed in 1979. The UNC, ANACH and FECORAH were among the founder members of FUNACAMH, but left alleging that left-wingers were subverting the organisation.

There is a proliferation of smaller peasant organisations, including the Asociación Campesina para el Desarrollo Agropecuario (ACADH), a 1979 split from ANACH with about 2,000 members; the Alianza Campesina de Organizaciones Nacionales de Honduras (ALCONH), a 1980 right-wing split from ANACH headed by the defeated candidate in ANACH's 1980 elections, Reyes Rodríguez, which is now linked to the National Party, with 1,500 members; and the Asociación Campesina Nacional (ACAN), a right-wing split from the UNC, which opposed UNC's entry into FUNACAMH.

There are two main women's peasant organisations: the Federación Hondureña de Mujeres Campesinas (FEHMUC), a Christian Democrat women's organisation formed in 1977, with around 5,000 members and 300 groups; and the Asociación Nacional de Mujeres Campesinas (ANAMUC), the ANACH women's organisation.

TEACHERS UNIONS

The two most important are the **Colegio Profesional Superior Magisterial Hondureño (COLPROSUMAH)** and the **Colegio de Profesores de Educación Media de Honduras (COPEMH)** who have formed the progressive Teachers' Unity Front (FUM).

HUMAN RIGHTS ORGANISATIONS

There are two human rights organisations, the **Committee for the Defence of Human Rights (CODEH)**, formed in 1981 and with Dr Ramón Custodio as president, and the **Committee of the Families of the Detained-Disappeared (COFADEH)**, formed in 1982 and with Zenaída Velásquez as president.

At the end of 1984 the CCOP (Comité Coordinadora de Organizaciones Populares — Coordinating Committee of Popular Organisations) was formed. It included the FUTH, CODEH, FUM, CNTC and various university and secondary student organisations.

13

List of Abbreviations

ACASCH	Asociación Campesina Social-Cristiana de Honduras / Social-Christian Peasant Association of Honduras.
AFL-CIO	American Federation of Labor — Congress of Industrial Organisations.
AIFLD	American Institute for Free Labor Development.
ALIPO	Alianza Liberal del Pueblo / People's Liberal Alliance.
ANACH	Asociación Nacional de Campesinos Hondureños / National Association of Honduran Peasants.
APROH	Asociación para el Progreso de Honduras / Association for the Progress of Honduras.
CACM	Central American Common Market.
CGT	Central General de Trabajadores / General Congress of Workers.
CLAT	Central Latinoamericana de Trabajadores / Latin American Confederation of Workers.
CNTC	Central Nacional de los Trabajadores del Campo / National Congress of Rural Workers.
CODEH	Comité para la Defensa de Derechos Humanos / Committee for the Defence of Human Rights.
COFADEH	Comité de las Familias de los Detenidos-Desaparecidos Hondureños / Committee of the Families of the Detained-Disappeared of Honduras.
COHEP	Consejo Hondureño de la Empresa Privada / Confederation of Honduran Private Business.
COLPROSUMAH	Colegio Profesional Superior Magisterial Hondureño / Honduran College of Teachers in Higher Education.
CONADI	Corporación Nacional de Inversiones / State Investment Corporation.
COPEMH	Colegio de Profesores de Educación Media de Honduras / Honduran College of Middle School Teachers.
COSUFA	Consejo Superior de las Fuerzas Armadas / Armed Forces' Superior Council.
CREM	Centro Regional de Entrenamiento Militar

14

	/ Regional Military Training Centre.
CTH	Confederación de Trabajadores de Honduras / Confederation of Honduran Workers.
CUS	Comité de Unidad Sindical / Trade Union Unity Committee.
DNI	Departamento Nacional de Investigaciones / National Department of Investigations.
FECESITLIH	Federación Central de Sindicatos Libres Hondureños / Central Federation of Honduran Free Trade Unions.
FECORAH	Federación de Cooperativas de la Reforma Agraria / Federation of Agrarian Reform Cooperatives.
FENACH	Federación Nacional de Campesinos Hondureños / National Federation of Honduran Peasants.
FENAGH	Federación Nacional de Agricultores y Ganaderos Hondureños / National Federation of Honduran Farmers and Cattle-raisers.
FESITRANH	Federación de Sindicatos de Trabajadores Norteños de Honduras / Northern Trade Union Federation of Honduran Workers.
FMLN	Frente Farabundo Martí para la Liberación Nacional / Farabundo Martí National Liberation Front.
FMLNH	Frente Morazanista de Liberación Nacional de Honduras / Honduran Morazanist National Liberation Front.
FPH	Frente Patriótico Hondureño / Honduran Patriotic Front.
FPR	Fuerzas Populares Revolucionarias 'Lorenzo Zelaya' / Popular Revolutionary Forces.
FSH	Federación Sindical Hondureña / Honduran Union Federation.
FUNACAMH	Frente de Unidad Nacional de Campesinos Hondureños / National Unity Front of Honduran Peasants.
FUNC	Frente de Unidad Campesina / Peasant Unity Front.
FUSEP	Fuerzas de Segúridad Pública / Public Security Forces.
FUTH	Federación Unitaria de Trabajadores de Honduras / United Federation of Workers.
MOLIDER	Movimiento Liberal Democrático Revolu-

	cionario / Revolutionary Democratic Liberal Movement.
MPL	Movimiento Popular de Liberación 'Cinchoneros' / 'Cinchoneros' Popular Liberation Movement.
ORIT	Organización Regional Interamericana del Trabajo / Inter-American Regional Organisation of Labor.
PASOH	Partido Socialista de Honduras / Honduran Socialist Party.
PCH	Partido Comunista de Honduras / Honduran Communist Party.
PCH/ML	Partido Comunista de Honduras-Marxista-Leninista / Honduran Communist Party (Marxist-Leninist).
PDCH	Partido Demócrata Cristiano de Honduras / Honduran Christian Democrat Party.
PINU	Partido de Innovación y Unidad / Innovation and Unity Party.
PRTC	Partido Revolucionario de los Trabajadores Centroamericanos / Revolutionary Party of Central American Workers.
SITRATERCO	Sindicato de Trabajadores de la Tela Railroad Company / Tela Railroad Company Workers' Union.
SITRASFRUCO	Sindicato de Trabajadores de Standard Fruit Company / Standard Fruit Company Workers' Union.
SUTRASFCO	Sindicato Unificado de Trabajadores de la Standard Fruit Company / Unified Union of Standard Fruit Company Workers.
STENEE	Sindicato de Trabajadores de la Empresa Nacional de Energía Eléctrica / Union of National Electric Energy Company.
UNC	Unión Nacional de Campesinos / National Union of Peasants.
UNCAH	Unión Nacional de Campesinos Auténticos Hondureños / National Union of Authentic Honduran Peasant Unions.
USAID	United States Agency for International Development.

2 From Independence to Dictatorship

'No Man's Land'

Of all the Central American states, Honduras has most claim to the label 'banana republic'. Since the turn of the century, its economy has been primarily dependent on the export of the 'green gold', while its political history has been shaped by the profiteering and corrupt practices of the fruit companies. Yet the term 'banana republic' also points to the absence of any Honduran national identity. For this, the North American companies do not bear sole responsibility. Even before their arrival, Honduras was hardly a nation at all. For the greater part of its history Honduras has been an ill-defined 'no man's land'. As one historian wrote recently, 'Everyone knew there was an entity called Honduras, but nobody knew where it was.'

The Mayan civilisation which covered large areas of Mexico and Guatemala from AD250-900 left its mark on Honduras only in the border area with Guatemala. The impressive ruins of the city of Copán, covering some 20 square kilometres, are a testament to the sophistication of Mayan intellectual and artistic achievement. But by the time of Columbus' arrival in 1502 the city had already been abandoned to the jungle. At the time of the conquest, Honduras was inhabited by a variety of Indian peoples, including the culturally and linguistically distinct *lenca* Indians in the western half of Honduras.

Spain succeeded in gaining control of the area in the 1540s, after a series of native rebellions nearly drove the invaders out of the country, such as the one led by the *lenca* chief, Lempira (later to give his name to the Honduran currency), in 1537. The discovery of gold and silver deposits briefly attracted the attention of the colonial power in the sixteenth century, but their significance soon paled in comparison to the richer deposits in Peru and Mexico. Honduras remained a backwater for most of the colonial period.

17

Nonetheless, it was through mining that the region established some identity of its own. Diseases brought in by the colonists in the first years of colonialism had virtually wiped out Honduras' tiny indigenous population, but in the latter part of the sixteenth century migrants from other parts of Central America were attracted to the mining towns of Tegucigalpa and Comayagua. Mining, in turn, stimulated local agriculture as cattle-raisers in particular found markets for their meat and dairy products. But in the seventeenth and eighteenth centuries silver exploration declined and subsistence agriculture became the core of Honduras' economy. With the main economic activities located elsewhere in Central America, Honduras was never much more than an appendage to the colonial political structures centred in Guatemala and Mexico.

But the ripples of the Independence movement, which were slowly affecting the rest of Central America, eventually reached Honduras. The United Provinces of Central America — a federal state which brought together modern Nicaragua, Costa Rica, El Salvador, Guatemala and Honduras — emerged in 1823. Most Central Americans had neither actively desired nor fought for independence, and within the United Provinces a substantial body of opinion remained loyal to Spain. The pro-federation forces under the Honduran general, Francisco Morazán, were finally defeated in 1838, and the federation soon dissolved into the five modern republics which have lasted to the present day.

The Absent Oligarchy

In most of the new republics, it was the consolidation of coffee as an export crop in the latter half of the nineteenth century that brought their economies firmly into the world market. The coffee boom had a number of important social and political effects, in particular the emergence of a powerful elite of coffee growers, who gave some semblance of national identity to the fledgling states. The process was not uniform in each republic. It depended on the geography and social composition of each state, and also on the ebb and flow of political battles between conservatives and liberals. The liberals sought free trade, the breakup of Indian communal lands and a reduction in the power of the church. Where they came to power, they carried through the far-reaching changes which helped consolidate the power of the coffee oligarchies.

The purest example of what is known as the 'Liberal revolution' took place in Guatemala, where Liberals came to power in 1871. Here, large numbers of Indian peasants were forced off their old communal lands to create a new class of landless agricultural workers providing plentiful labour for coffee plantations. Even those who retained smallholdings *(minifundia)* were obliged by law to pick coffee during the harvest season. At the same time, railways and roads were built to encourage trade, and a modern army and police force were established to consolidate the new order. This system of centralised government facilitated the development of a modern nation state.

However, conditions in Honduras were different and what happened in Guatemala was only partially repeated. The distinction is central to an understanding of the subsequent economic and political development of Honduras. Coffee did not become a major export until the 1940s, while banana production, the major export crop until then, soon came under foreign control. In contrast to Guatemala, a strong national elite linked to profitable coffee exports did not emerge in Honduras in the nineteenth century. The state remained weak as competing elites, none of them strong enough to impose complete authority, fought a series of internal battles for power.

The inaccessibility of many areas and the power of regional landowners over the peasant population strengthened local autonomy. In the absence of any centralised national authority, frequent civil wars were the dominant feature of the post-independence period. Between 1821 and 1876, 85 different presidents ruled Honduras — one general, José María Medina, is said to have taken control on eleven separate occasions. When major political change did come to Honduras, once again it did not evolve from any internal dynamic. The Liberal rebels who took power in 1876 relied on Guatemalan support. The two Hondurans who led the uprising — Aurelio Soto and Ramón Rosa — had served under the Guatemalan president, General Barrios. Soto and Ramos did not represent the rise to power of a new Honduran agro-exporting elite but championed a model imported from Guatemala. The two duly started the reform process by abolishing church taxes and establishing a number of incentives to encourage the same sort of export-led growth that had occurred in Guatemala.

But, for a number of reasons, Honduras' attempt at Liberal reform failed to evolve in the same way as in El Salvador and Guatemala. First, Soto and Ramos were unable to stimulate a coffee boom. Ecologically, parts of Honduras could have produced coffee, as developments since the 1940s have demonstrated. But in the 1870s, relatively few farmers grew coffee with any commercial success. This was partly due to labour shortages. Unlike its Guatemalan and Salvadorean counterparts, the Honduran Liberal government left the *ejidos* (land owned by municipalities and rented out to peasants) and other communal forms of land tenure largely intact. This maintained

19

stability in the rural areas for many years, but in the short term it acted as an obstacle to coffee production. A second factor was the absence of an infrastructure for marketing coffee. In Guatemala and El Salvador, where geographical conditions were easier, this had been established early on for the trade in dyestuffs which preceded coffee, giving both countries a relatively extensive road and communications network. In addition, a number of merchants in Guatemala City and San Salvador had greater experience of the world market and a wide range of contacts abroad. Along with the large landowners they had accumulated profits in the dyestuffs trade, which they could now invest in coffee. In Honduras, by contrast, landowners were short of capital and often isolated geographically. When they did try to sell their coffee to Europe, they found themselves without the necessary commercial contacts.

Secondly, Honduran Liberals took over a government which was heavily indebted, which limited the amount of capital available for building roads and railways. The cost of constant warfare had exhausted reserves, but more importantly, between 1867 and 1870 Honduras had contracted four loans from Britain worth £6 million to build a railway linking its Pacific and Atlantic coasts. By 1873 Honduras had defaulted on all four loans, and over the next 50 years the debt rose 500 per cent to around £30 million. Honduran government officials proved hopelessly corrupt. Only 55 miles of the railway were ever built and to this day, Honduras' capital, Tegucigalpa, remains one of the few in the world without a railway. Successive governments were shackled with a debt which was not finally paid off until 1953.

Soto and Ramos did succeed in establishing a central statistical office, setting up telegraphic communication with the US and reorganising public finances, but Honduras did not have a central bank or its own currency until 1950. Only in one respect did the achievements of Honduran Liberalism match those of its neighbours — the success which its generous foreign concessions had in attracting foreign investment. Soto and subsequent Liberal presidents, following the example of President Barrios, were anxious to attract capital from abroad. In the last two decades of the nineteenth century a number of concessions were granted to regenerate silver mining. British, German and US capital was drawn into the country, and by the end of the century silver accounted for 50 per cent of exports. Although a small group of native Hondurans did benefit from this wealth, they were completely dependent on foreign capital.

In Honduras, the power of foreign interests was not counter-balanced by a strong class of agrarian capitalists, as it was in Guatemala. Thus, while the modest reforms of the Liberals gave the government only minimal control over its own economic affairs, they allowed foreign capital to gain control of the modernised sector of the economy. Honduras was independent in name only, and was extraordinarily vulnerable to the dynamic expansion of US capitalism that took place at the beginning of the twentieth century. No other Central American state was as weak. The conditions were firmly established for the country's historical subservience to North American interests.

The Arrival of the Banana Companies

Britain had been the major foreign power in Central America since Independence. Its merchant fleets, backed by a powerful navy, won considerable advantage from the expansion of trade which accompanied Independence, and during the first half of the nineteenth century the British consolidated their hold over the Atlantic side of the isthmus. British Honduras (Belize) became the major entrepôt for Central American trade. While the British military occupied the Bay Islands off Honduras' Atlantic coast and Greytown (San Juan del Norte) in Nicaragua, British investors made loans to Honduras and other Central American states on ruinous terms which the British government was often prepared to protect by force.

However, from the mid nineteenth century Britain found itself faced with growing problems in Europe, and its influence began to wane as that of the US grew. The American Civil War greatly strengthened the economic power of northern manufacturers who were able to take advantage of the foreign concessions offered by Liberal governments throughout Central America. Britain remained the major foreign investor in Central America during the nineteenth century, but US investment gradually increased and by the end of the century equalled that of the British. At the same time, US naval power in the Caribbean and Pacific grew to match British strength. The construction of the Panama canal in 1914 and a series of military interventions throughout Central America (including Honduras in 1911 and 1912) confirmed US control of the area. The US succeeded in replacing Britain as the dominant power in the region.

The growth of US influence in Honduras was closely related to the expansion of a number of fruit companies which at the turn of the century were attracted to the rich agricultural belt along the country's north coast. In the last three decades of the nineteenth century, local farmers had found American traders eager to buy their bananas. Trade was limited by the difficulties of transporting a fruit which rots relatively quickly, but the introduction of refrigeration at the end of

21

the century revolutionised the industry, opening up huge new markets in the US and Europe. Demand grew enough to make direct investment in production attractive to US entrepreneurs, who were soon able to buy out local Honduran rivals and win an increasing share of a growing trade. Honduran governments welcomed these developments and, in the belief that an influx of foreign capital would have beneficial spin-offs for the whole of the economy and society, extended generous concessions to the banana companies. Companies were exempted from paying custom duties, were given mineral and other rights over land and were allowed to build and control railways, canals, ports, finance centres and import/export houses.

Two companies took centre stage: in the east around the port of La Ceiba, it was the Vaccaro brothers (who were subsequently to become Standard Fruit), and to the west, along the banks of the Cuyamel river and near the port of Tela, Samuel Zemurray (commonly known as 'Sam the banana man') set up the Cuyamel Fruit Company. From 1912 onwards a third force emerged. The United Fruit Company, through its two subsidaries the Tela and Trujillo Railroad Companies, took over some of Zemurray's properties to the east of Cuyamel and then totally swallowed up Zemurray's creation in 1929. The banana industry grew rapidly. Bananas accounted for 11 per cent of total exports in 1892, 42 per cent in 1903 and 66 per cent in 1913. Production increased from around six million branches in 1910 to 30 milion in 1929. Foreign control of the industry was virtually complete — by 1918, 75 per cent of banana lands were owned by the three companies.

The companies were zealous in their attempts to secure the most favourable concessions (see box, p.23). They promised to build railways linking the capital to the banana growing areas, but the mileage actually laid was little more than what was strictly necessary for the smooth running of their operations. The railways tended to run parallel to the sea and not towards Tegucigalpa. In addition, in return for each kilometre of railway built, the companies received huge land concessions in lots adjacent to the railway. The terms of the concessions also included a provision that local farmers should own alternate lots of land as a way of retaining a certain degree of local control over the industry. But companies soon found that they could by-pass these provisions by buying off local landowners. It was not long before they owned northern Honduras.

The banana boom did provide the export-led growth so desired by the Liberals. But whereas the coffee boom and the rise of the coffee bourgeoisies elsewhere in Central America had brought some semblance of national development, in Honduras the banana boom actually impeded development. In Guatemala and El Salvador, strong

The Rolston Letter

Cortés Development Company,
Puerto Cortés
20 July 1920

Dr Luis Melara
San Pedro Sula

Dear Luis,

1. In order that our great sacrifices and numerous investments have not been made in vain, we must take possession of as much state-owned and private land as possible, and acquire as much wealth as we have the capacity and power to absorb.

2. We must take every opportunity to enrich our company, and secure every possibility of exploiting new areas of operations. In short, we must acquire every piece of land that seems in accordance with our strategic interests and which guarantees our future progress and agricultural development, thus increasing our economic power.

3. We must draw up such irreversible contracts that nobody can compete with us, not even in the distant future; our aim is to ensure that whatever other company manages to establish itself and develop its operations, it will always fall under our control and adapt itself to our established principles.

4. We must secure concessions, privileges and exemptions from tariffs and custom duties; we must free ourselves of all public taxes and all those obligations and responsibilities which reduce our earnings and those of our associates. We must build for ourselves a privileged position with the aim of imposing our commercial philosophy and defending our economic interests.

5. It is indispensable to capture the imagination of these subjugated peoples, and attract them to the idea of our aggrandisement, and in a general way to those politicians and bosses that we must use. Observation and careful study have assured us that a people degraded by drink can be assimilated to the demands of necessity and destiny; it is in our interest to make it our concern that the privileged class, whom we will need for our exclusive benefit, bend itself to our will; in general, none of them has any conviction or character, far less patriotism; they seek only position and rank, and on being granted them, we will make them hungry for even more.

> 6. These men must not act on their own initiative, but rather according to determining factors and under our immediate control.
>
> 7. We must distance ourselves from those of our friends who have been in our service; we must consider them as degraded by their loyalty because sooner or later they will betray us; we must distance ourselves from those who feel offended and treat them with some deference, without being of any use to them. We do need their country, the natural resources of their coasts and ports, and little by little we must acquire them . . .
>
> We are then at the point of departure; you know these men better than I. On your arrival, I will show you a list of the land we must obtain, if possible, immediately . . .
>
> Until we meet,
>
> H.V. Rolston

state institutions had emerged and the Pacific coastal ports were integrated with the capital cities and centres of agricultural production. In Honduras, investment was concentrated on the northern Atlantic coast, which remained geographically and economically isolated from the agricultural zones of southern and central Honduras. The effect of economic growth in the north on these backward areas was minimal, as the banana economy functioned virtually autonomously.

An excellent network of roads and railways — owned by affiliates of the banana companies — linked San Pedro Sula, Tela and La Ceiba, but all three towns still remained isolated from the capital. The result was that it easier to travel from Tela to New Orleans than from Tela to Tegucigalpa. The banana companies imported almost everything, including equipment for their ports and railways, and consumer goods for company shops. A large part of the labour demand was met by bringing in workers from the labour surplus countries of the Caribbean, Mexico and El Salvador. Workers were made dependent on the company for all their provisions by a system of company tokens to be used only at company shops. So the north of Honduras functioned as an enclave economy. The banana lands were held purely as a source of wealth for the banana companies, and, with little or no customs or tax requirements, central government could gain little revenue. The nearest thing Honduras had to a state was the mini-version created by the companies in and around the plantations.

Company Power

The banana companies soon developed a level of political influence commensurate with their economic power. For this, they took advantage of the fact that the country's political system was as vulnerable as its underdeveloped economy. After the overthrow of Aurelio Soto in 1883, constant civil wars between liberals and conservatives lasted for 50 years until 1933. The endemic political instability was accentuated by the rivalry between the major banana companies who sought Honduran allies in the political parties in order to extract the best concessions.

Honduras' two political parties reflected the weakness of the local ruling elite. Although the origins of both the Liberal and National parties are obscure, the two-party system probably stems from the battles between the conservative clerics and liberal anti-clerics in the post-independence period. While the Liberals emerged with a formal constitution in the 1890s, the Nationalists were slower to appear as a coherent group. Its formation owed something to the old clerical conservatives, but more to the response of a faction of the Liberals who felt that they had not enjoyed their fair share of office. The National party received judicial status in 1916, but it was not until 1923 that Tiburcio Carías Andino (himself a former member of the Liberal party) pulled together the various factions of the party behind his candidacy for the presidency.

Membership of either party depended on a complex mix of regional and personal loyalties, not on ideological or economic differences. Nationalists were every bit as in favour of foreign investment as their Liberal rivals, and both parties were equally conservative on social issues. The two-party system was simply a vehicle in a spoils system and parties used their control of government to bestow patronage, often in the form of jobs, to their supporters. This tradition has lasted to the present day.

A political crisis between 1911 and 1912 demonstrated the power the companies soon wielded over the two parties. In 1911, President Dávila's government had foolishly shown too much favour towards United Fruit, so Zemurray's Cuyamel company organised a mercenary force, led by a soldier of fortune named Lee Christmas, to oust him. The invasion failed, but in order to restore stability, the US stepped in to negotiate Dávila's replacement. The new president, Manuel Bonilla, soon granted Zemurray more concessions, while Zemurray showed his gratitude by negotiating a loan to help Bonilla pay the bill for the invasion that had brought him to power. Lee Christmas also received his reward — he later became US consul in Honduras.

In Quest of a Railway

The National Railway runs through the world's best banana lands; its control was the lever to their domination. Cuyamel made sure that the railway would not return to the government in a great hurry. Though Honduran law prohibited the building of private railroads in a zone forty kilometres on either side of the National Railway, Cuyamel proceeded to construct clandestine lines in the Choloma, San Pedro Sula, and Villanueva districts. Eventually it laid a railway along the Ulua River, directly parallel to the National Railway, to syphon off its traffic and revenues.

After a destructive three-cornered civil war in 1924, the Nationalist Miguel Paz Barahona became president. In general, Cuyamel was backing the Liberals while United Fruit was betting on the Nationalist horse. President Paz Barahona, however, was estranged from the bulk of his party and soon found himself in Cuyamel's harness. The great issue that agitated Honduran politics of the period was the legalisation of Cuyamel's 'clandestine lines'. Mercenary journalists, retained by one or the other of the fruit companies, were debating the issue in the press with heat and histrionics. President Paz Barahona was exerting himself to have the lines sanctified, while the president of Congress, Tiburcio Carías Andino, was blocking the move on orders from United Fruit. On the outcome of the fight hinged Cuyamel's continued control of the National Railway and the rich acres flanking it. Money circulated freely. It was during this time that Zemurray spoke his winged phrase: 'In Honduras a mule costs more than a deputy.'

Alfredo Schlesinger, a talented Guatemalan publicist of Austro-Hungarian origins, achieved the unusual feat of serving both Cuyamel and its arch-foe Carías at the same time. In 1927, on his way back from a lobbying mission in Washington on Carías's behalf, he met Zemurray in New Orleans and received the following instructions: 'We are going to have Congress convoked to grant us a concession legalising the clandestine lines. Now, I want you to go and tell Carías that either Congress approves the concession, or we will never let him become president. We will spend all the money necessary to prevent it.'

Source: William Krehm, *Democracies and Tyrannies of the Caribbean*, Lawrence Hill and Company, 1984.

After 1912, internal Honduran politics became virtually indistinguishable from the activities of the fruit companies, in particular the rivalries between Cuyamel and United Fruit. Zemurray and Cuyamel developed close links with the Liberal Party while United Fruit allied with the National Party. Politicians were kept on company payrolls and arms were shipped and financed for rival groups of insurgents. Presidents came to power and fell from grace depending on the favours and money of the fruit companies (see box opposite). The companies' political and economic clout made the Honduran elite even weaker. It was never to possess the wealth, the vision nor the rigid political control of the landowning oligarchies of El Salvador and Guatemala. As early as 1920, United Fruit's H.V. Rolston showed remarkable vision in describing its essential characteristics. In a letter to his lawyer, he wrote that of '. . . this privileged class, whom we need for our exclusive benefit . . . none of them has any convictions or character, far less patriotism'.

The Doctor and General

Following the Wall Street crash in 1929, commodity prices tumbled and markets contracted sharply. In Central America both the coffee planters and banana growers rationalised their operations, creating rapid increases in unemployment and imposing wage cuts. In El Salvador, Guatemala, Nicaragua and Honduras, the agrarian oligarchies turned to a series of ruthless — and eccentric — dictators to maintain the economic and social status quo and resolve the crisis of the 1930s.

In El Salvador, when discontent among the peasantry grew alarmingly in the early 1930s, the oligarchy turned to the military to maintain their economic power intact. The vegetarian theosophist Colonel Maximiliano Hernández Martínez commanded a massacre of over 30,000 rebellious peasants in 1932, and remained in power until 1944. In Guatemala, the motorcycling enthusiast General Jorge Ubico came to power in 1932, and executed 100 labour, student and opposition leaders. For the next 12 years, Guatemala was, according to one contemporary observer, 'as orderly as an empty billiard table'. In Nicaragua, the crisis was most successfully resolved in 1936 by the imposition of the first of the Somozas, Anastasio I. When the US marines departed in 1933, they left behind the National Guard as their trained surrogates, who remained as the ultimate guarantors of the Somoza dynasty until its overthrow in 1979.

Honduras too had its dictator. *'El Doctor y General'*, Tiburcio Carías Andino, had earned the first half of his title when the Liberal government of 1907 rewarded him with an honorary law degree for his part in the rebellion that had brought them to power. The length of his legal career — one case fought and lost — was soon outstripped by his 16 years of dictatorship.

In Honduras also, the depression was initially accompanied by an increase in working-class militancy on the banana plantations. In 1932 a strike among the banana workers organised by the Communist-dominated Honduran Union Federation (FSH), threatened social unrest. But although Carías was soon to kill and jail a number of labour leaders and destroy all labour organisations, popular organisation was very weak and posed no real threat to the establishment. As a result, Carías was less severe than Hernández Martínez or Ubico. According to one contemporary journalist, he 'affected the role of a heavy-handed patriarch rather than a sadistic dictator'.

Gradually, the ending of the rivalry between the banana companies opened up the possibility of greater political stability in Honduras. In 1929 Zemurray sold Cuyamel to United Fruit for US$32 million, and thus brought to an end to the company-backed civil wars that had plagued Honduras through the 1920s. Revolts continued after 1929, but they no longer had a fruit company behind them to give them muscle. With the near-complete monopolisation of the banana industry by United Fruit after 1929, Carías' National Party was able to rely on the company for its political dominance and source of patronage. Government officials were on United's payrolls and the country's political elites saw United Fruit as the main source of finance for the national budget. The Liberals inevitably declined without the financial support from Cuyamel.

The most serious threat to Carías' rule came with the Liberal revolt in November 1932 after Carías' electoral triumph. But helped by arms from the Salvadorean government and two planes from a New Zealander named Lowell Yerex, the rebels were soon routed. Carías immediately took the offensive, exiling Liberal leaders and closing down the opposition press. After 1933 elections were abolished and Carías had his presidential term extended until 1939 and subsequently until 1948. In his later years he was able to exhibit a certain degree of political flexibility. Having first banned baseball in case the bats could be used in any conspiracy against him, he was persuaded by his nephew (a lover of the sport) to legalise it on the grounds that pitching would be useful for soldiers learning how to throw hand grenades.

3 New Actors Emerge

By extending the organisation of the National Party to the most remote areas of the republic, Carías had brought a semblance of national unity to Honduras for the first time. Nevertheless, by 1945 Honduras still remained the most backward and dependent of the Central American states, with its economy consisting of large banana plantations along the northern coast and an underdeveloped agricultural sector throughouth the rest of the country. Outside the banana enclaves, large landowners and small peasant farmers produced livestock, basic grains and a few export crops such as coffee and tobacco. The landowning elites and the banana companies were still the dominant political forces. The country's infrastructure was very much as it had been in the nineteenth century (San Pedro Sula and Tegucigalpa, Honduras' largest cities, were not connected by paved roads until the 1950s), while the national economy still functioned without a central bank or income tax system.

However, in the years following the second world war, Honduras embarked on a limited economic programme of diversification and modernisation. Gradually, a more dynamic and business-oriented agricultural sector emerged, along with the beginnings of a mercantile and professional middle class. The working class made its first decisive appearance on the political stage with the biggest labour action in Honduran history. Finally, the Honduran military entered the scene, starting a long tradition of military domination of Honduran politics. The net result was that the old political nexus of the banana companies and the conservative landowners was threatened and subsequently replaced by a more varied group of political actors. All these developments were accompanied by changes in the traditional form of economic and political dependency. The powerful, but more subtle influence of the US government and its agencies (US training for the army, control by US labour

29

organisations over the Honduran union movement, and US economic aid programmes) were substituted for the crude wheelings and dealings of the banana companies.

Political and Economic Diversification

The second world war changed the political and economic face of Central America. Before the war, the dictators — Ubico, Hernández Martínez, Carías and Somoza — had all been sympathetic to European fascism, but the eventual victory of the Allied forces brought the whole region decisively under US influence. The constant anti-fascist and democratic rhetoric undermined the dictators' political hold, and in 1944 Ubico and Hernández Martínez were overthrown by loose alliances of middle class professional groups, students and junior officers. At the same time, the economic settlement which followed the war opened new markets and new opportunities for both public and private investment.

In Honduras, Carías initially rode out protests both from Liberals and from rival members of his own National Party. But he soon came under increasing pressure from the banana companies and local elites, who saw his continued rule both as a threat to the country's fragile political consensus and as an obstacle to the creation of more modern economic institutions. In 1948 they finally forced him to stand down in favour of a moderate conservative and National Party politician, Juan Manuel Gálvez. International demand for new agricultural products and high world prices led the Gálvez government to initiate a series of economic measures which stimulated capitalist development in previously untouched areas of the Honduran countryside. The state apparatus was expanded and began to provide the infrastructure and financial and technical assistance (mostly from US sources) that was necessary if the economy was to take advantage of the boom in the world economy.

Acting on the advice of a World Bank mission which visited Honduras in 1950, Gálvez established a National Development Bank (BANAFOM) and a Central Bank, giving the government some control over the economy for the first time. Funds were made available for a series of public works, such as new roads and bridges, and new lines of credit were channelled into cotton-growing in the south, cattle-raising and sugar cultivation in the north, and some coffee-growing on small and medium-sized farms in the highland regions. In the banana enclaves, the fruit companies also began a moderate programme of diversification. Although United Fruit

Land, Work and Profits

● In 1930 United Fruit's landed empire totalled 3,482,042 acres, thus constituting an international farm equal to the combined area of Connecticut and Rhode Island in the US [or of Northern Ireland].[1]

● Stock dividends have multiplied by 7½ the original investments of all who owned ten or more shares in 1900. Each holder of one hundred shares in 1899 . . . should have received US$58,959 in 33¼ years, or an average income of approximately 17¾ per cent p.a. on his investment of US$10,000.[1]

● During 1922 the average monthly earnings per labourer in a new Honduran district, to which it was necessary to attract workers, was about US$45 a month. During 1925, however, in another Honduran district, where labour was more plentiful, the average monthly earnings per labourer were less than US$24.[1]

● During the period from 1925 to 1950 . . . the banana companies sent back to their headquarters a remarkable US$412.5 million in profits, which means a yearly average of US$16.5 million. From 1912 until 1955 the Honduran state exempted the banana companies from paying US$120,806,000 . . . If the state had charged the banana companies what they did not pay because of their exemptions, the country could have increased its income by 50 per cent.[2]

● Labourers' camps are built of rough boards, generally with corrugated iron roofs having no ceiling under them, and are elevated on stilts. Some of them are one-room houses, many of them two-room two-family houses, and others are long drawn-out tenements, sliced off with partitions every twelve feet for each family. They are decidedly overcrowded. Entire families occupy single rooms about twelve foot square.[1]

● Examination of 2,248 labourers in Honduras in 1930, conducted by the Cortés Development Company, revealed that the percentage of malarial infection of workers living in screened camps was 15.21 per cent, while that of those in unscreened camps was 31.81 per cent.[1]

● 'There is an air of dreaminess about them that verges on apathy, as they lounge in front of their camps. The insidious laziness is induced by impoverished blood, where the plasmodia of malaria have been playing havoc . . . They lie in their hammocks, smoking and looking at the sky; they sit on the railroad tracks, and grunt as approaching trains disturb their repose.' (Report by Dr José A. López of the United Fruit Company's hospital at Puerto Castilla, 1930.)[1]

31

- Each worker has an average of one accident a year, with most occurring during the cutting process. Many also suffer chronic health problems. Those who stand in the packing sheds all day are commonly afflicted with circulatory diseases, and many who wash and spray the fruit with chemicals suffer a persistent fungus on their hands. During harvest days . . . those who do the cutting and packing often work twelve-hour days, from five o'clock in the morning to five o'clock at night. For the workers who cut and carry 100- to 150-pound banana stems laden with fruit, the result is often muscular disorders, not to speak of constant exhaustion. It is no wonder that these workers have a useful plantation life of about twelve years.[3]

Sources:
(1) C.D. Kepner Jr, *Social Aspects of the Banana Industry,* Columbia University Press, 1936. (2) V. Carías and V. Meza, *Las compañías bananeras en Honduras: un poco de historia.* (3) R. Burbach and P. Flynn, *Agribusiness in the Americas,* Monthly Review Press, 1980.

expanded its total area of cultivation from 82,000 acres in 1946 to 133,000 acres in 1953, the amount of land dedicated to bananas actually fell. The companies expanded operations to include cattle-raising and the production of such crops as *abacá* (a type of hemp), African palm oil and cacao.

The economic changes led to a slow change in the nature of the Honduran elites. With the expansion of the various agro-exports and the slow development of an industrial sector, a new group of local entrepreneurs emerged whose interests were not automatically represented by the old paternalistic style of the traditional parties. At the same time, the overthrow of Ubico in Guatemala and a new international climate encouraged moderate radicalisation in the incipient urban middle class, which also increased pressure for a political opening. Small parties such as the Honduran Democratic Revolutionary Party (PDRH) were formed outside the traditional political spectrum.

The Liberal Party had taken a long time to recover from the take-over of Cuyamel by United Fruit in 1929. Bankrupt and marginalised under Carías, the party eventually began to pick up support from among these new groups which emerged after the second world war, and in particular the urban professional class. A fresh leadership around Ramón Villeda Morales identified with the modernising and social-democratic ideologies being advanced by politicians like José Figueres in Costa Rica, and attempted to break with the party's rural landowning base and *caudillo* traditions. The Liberal Party eventually came to power in 1957, but not before the Honduran working class and military had also emerged as significant political actors.

The Rise of the Working Class

It was within the labour movement that the most momentous political events were to take place. The moderate liberalisation under Gálvez had given the workers a chance to organise to greater effect, and in 1954 some 50,000 workers went on strike, mostly in the north of Honduras. Such is the importance of the strike that many Honduran analysts argue that their country's history did not really begin until 1954. The success of the strike secured for Honduran workers the right to form trade unions. But it also heralded the involvement of US labour organisations, in particular ORIT (the Inter-American Regional Organisation of Labor) and AIFLD (the American Institute for Free Labor Development), in the Honduran labour movement. Radical union leaders were ousted as unions fell under the influence of US policies for labour control.

But, in fact, Honduran labour history began long before 1954. Tegucigalpa's petty traders, tailors, carpenters and small artisans formed Honduras' first trade unions at the turn of the century. But these were sectorally based mutual associations lacking any working-class identity. The first class-based unions emerged on the northern coast among the banana workers. It was here on Cuyamel's banana plantations that Honduras' first recorded strike occurred in 1916. Workers struck again in 1917 and 1918, prompting Cuyamel's owner, Sam Zemurray, to import non-unionised labour from the Caribbean. By 1928, the majority of the banana workers were members of the Honduran Union Federation (FSH).

The FSH organised a series of strikes on the banana plantations in 1929, and in 1930 martial law was declared on the northern coast. Despite the imprisonment and deportation of a number of FSH leaders, the strike movement continued in 1931 and early 1932. It finally ended when the newly elected President Carías declared a state of siege in the banana zone and employed a paramilitary force, the White Guard, to intimidate and beat up FSH members and supporters. The most militant workers were seized, flown to El Salvador and left there. But the movement never posed a serious threat to Honduras' stability. Geographically isolated, the FSH was easily out-manoeuvred.

The end of the Carías period saw a degree of liberalisation inside the banana belt and some reformist unions in the cities were tolerated. But in the economically powerful banana empire, little changed. The

United Fruit banana plantation.

companies had a highly efficient machine of political control. Company watchmen and 'shop-guards' worked with military commanders to silence trade union organisers, while a system of patronage based on promotion and wage increases fostered the growth of an extensive spy network.

The trade unions had to work in semi-clandestinity to survive. In such conditions, the small, disciplined and highly committed Communist Party thrived. It became the leading force behind the Trade Union Unity Committee (CUS), which from its base in El Progreso spearheaded the drive for both legal recognition and a substantial improvement in conditions. Their leadership, strengthened in April 1954 by the return of Communist exiles from Guatemala, was crucial to the remarkable general strike which shook Honduras in May 1954.

For what was to be the most extensive industrial and political action in Honduran history, the immediate grievances behind the strike seem minor. On Easter Sunday 1954, United Fruit's management refused to pay dockers at Puerto Cortés double time, whereupon the dockers stopped work. Strike actions spread: nurses in the company hospital and construction workers took action for pay increases. At the end of April, the strike mushroomed at a pace which its leaders could not have predicted. Soon all of United Fruit's plantations were affected, and then on 1 May, Standard Fruit workers came out in solidarity. In addition to a 50 per cent wage increase, the leaders now advanced what was to be the principal demand of the strike: the legal recognition of unions. Given that the fruit companies paid as much as one-fifth of all salaries in the country, workers knew that if they were successful, other employers would have to follow suit. The popularity of the demands drew the strikers moral and financial support from students, teachers, small tradesmen and intellectuals from all over Honduras. Peasant families gave food to the striking families, and radio broadcasts from Guatemala urged the workers to stand firm. With 50,000 workers on strike, all the northern ports were crippled, the banana enclave ground to a halt and communications with Tegucigalpa were cut.

Given this remarkable display of the workers' power, it was surprising that the strike was broken without recourse to the unmitigated repression characteristic of labour relations elsewhere in Central America. Indeed, the way the strike was ended had a good deal more impact on the subsequent history of the Honduran labour movement than its actual achievements.

By 28 May, just over a month after the strike had begun, a number of weaknesses in the movement became apparent. On 19 May, the Standard Fruit management met their workers' demands for a series

The Green Prison

In the midst of a dense undergrowth of brambles, reeds and tall grasses that choked the abandoned banana fields, the clearers made their machetes whistle through the air as, bent double and breathing noisily like cattle, they hacked their way through the tangle. Clouds of thistledown flew up and settled again, sticking into their reddened, sweaty skin as they plodded along like sleepwalkers, heavy with weariness and enervation.

Elsewhere, the gang of planters drilled the dark, heavy earth with their 'dibbers', irresistible battering rams in their iron fists, while their companions carried on their aching backs the long poles that had to be buried at the foot of the trees already bearing bunches to support them and protect them from the ceaseless east winds which swept the valley.

Here, a group was cutting the sturdy bunches, ash-grey with insecticide, that were to be carried by men and mules to the railway lines, where they would be dipped in a solution of hydrochloric acid and water and then loaded onto the fruit wagons.

C. Capa/Magnum

Over there, the waterers clambered up the ladders of the sprinklers and turned them on, sending the precious water gushing in a huge arc to soak the fertile earth and the plants that were already withering from a surfeit of sun. Down the valley, close to the river, others were at work on the irrigation channels, busy opening and shutting sluices. Soaked to the bone yet burnt up inside with fever, they lived up to the nickname of 'ducks' their colleagues had bestowed on them.

Further on, in the new land recently acquired from the local landowners, squads of labourers worked alongside the engineers, measuring and dividing up the ground, marking paths with lines of posts for the clearers and carriers, for the thousands of men without land, hut or bread who were caught up in this whirlwind stirred up by the fruit company.

And, amidst all this confusion of labourers and banana-trees, sun and pestilence, sweat and machines, creeks and malaria, rang out the cocky shouts of the foremen, the whistling of the overseers, and the arrogant, all-powerful gringo slang.

So it went on all day long. The peasants' exhausting toil stretched out until nightfall when, their legs buckling under them with weariness, they quit the green prison of the banana plantations only to be engulfed in the dispiriting prison of their soulless, barrack-like quarters.

Adapted from: Ramón Amaya Amador, *Prisión Verde,* Editorial Baktun, Tegucigalpa, 1983 (first published in Mexico in 1950). [Translation by Nick Caistor].

of improvements in conditions. United Fruit then found it easier to tackle its more militant strikers. Even here, though, the authorities opted for a combination of force and negotiation rather than outright repression. This is partly explained by the Honduran political situation in the summer of 1954.

Since assuming office, President Gálvez had distanced himself from the legacy of Carías and broken with the National Party, which he saw as an obstacle to further modernisation programmes. In the run-up to the elections of October 1954, his new party, the National Reformist Movement, aimed to present a reforming image which precluded hard-line repression of the strikers. At the same time, the US State Department had embarked on a more interventionist diplomacy throughout Latin America. It aimed to present a progressive and 'democratic' alternative to the growing influence of communist ideas in the region. The international federations of US labour organisations, and in particular the American Federation of Labor

(AFL), started to play a key role in US efforts to undermine the militancy of Latin American labour and gain control over the union movement. Honduras was an ideal testing ground for the policy. The fruit companies had accepted that unionisation was inevitable, while local elites were too weak to oppose them.

At the end of May 1954, amidst an atmosphere of deliberately whipped up anti-communist hysteria, the government arrested several strike committee leaders. This enabled a number of prominent anti-communists among the strikers who had been trained by ORIT to win control of the strike committee. At the same time, the AFL stepped up its diplomatic pressure on the companies to end the strike. The AFL's president, George Meany, told company executives that 'unless the position of those who defend the cause of democracy and liberty is reinforced, unions will fall into the hands of militant communists which would have disagreeable consequences for our country's position in Latin America.' La Lima, the United Fruit company town near San Pedro Sula, was the centre of the pro-US self-styled 'democratic' faction, which was financially supported by the US and could rely on police protection. The left fought rearguard actions at Puerto Cortés and El Progreso, but when the strikers' economic position began to deterioriate, pressure from the base built up for a settlement, which was finally reached on 8 July 1954.

Enter US Labour

The actual achievements of the strikers were mixed. Their biggest success was the recognition of the right to form trade unions, of which the most important was SITRATERCO, the United Fruit Workers' union. The agreement paved the way for a series of labour laws culminating in 1959 with the country's first labour code. Wage increases of 10 and 15 per cent were considerably less than the 50 per cent increases they had demanded, but the strikers did obtain paid holidays and improvements in medical provisions for themselves and their families.

However, by guaranteeing industrial peace, the settlement allowed the fruit companies to push through a process of rationalisation. A clause in the agreement signed by the workers at Standard had ambiguously stated that 'no closure or suspension of any of the company's operations is to be understood as a reprisal', which in effect gave the companies *carte blanche* to sack large numbers of workers. A series of natural disasters hastened the restructuring of the banana industry. In September 1954, the rivers Ulua, Chamelecón and

Comayagua flooded, damaging three-quarters of the Honduran banana plantations and forcing the companies to take 31 per cent of land out of production. An outbreak of Panama disease reduced production even further. But the settlement of the strike enabled the companies to mechanise their plantations and boost productivity in that way, without fear of labour unrest. The introduction of packing plants reduced labour requirements at the docks, while helicopters were used to spray the crops against diseases. The result was that thousands of banana workers were thrown out of their jobs. United Fruit employed 26,000 workers in 1954; over 10,000 were sacked in 1955 and by 1957 employment had fallen to 13,000. Between 1954 and 1959, Standard also fired about half of their workers. Although there was a 30 per cent increase in production from 1954 to 1959, a total of 19,000 workers lost their jobs during the same period.

Meanwhile, the pro-US leaders consolidated their grip on the Honduran trade union movement. SITRATERCO was the vanguard of US influence within the movement, and was to be an ORIT bulwark for the next 20 years. SITRATERCO's leaders were trained in the US, and from 1956 onwards its leaders propagated an anti-communist and pro-US view of the world. At the same time, USAID (the US government agency for international development) channelled large sums of money to a number of unions, including 90,000 lempiras (US$45,000) to build SITRATERCO's offices in La Lima. This flow of funds and the tacit support of the government allowed ORIT to wield enormous influence over the large number of new unions which formed after 1954.

Left-wing organisations, in particular the Communist Party, preserved some influence initially. In El Progreso, independents formed the Independent Union of Tela Railroad Workers, in Puerto Cortés the Tela Railroad Workers' Union, and in La Lima the Independent Mechanics' Union. But ORIT was influential in the formation of the Standard Fruit workers' union (SITRASFRUCO) in 1955, and elsewhere left-wing activists faced harassment from governments increasingly influenced by cold-war ideology. ORIT's US-trained leaders were responsible for shaping Honduras' first national confederations, the Northern Trade Union Federation of Honduran Workers (FESITRANH) in 1957, and a year later its equivalent in the south, FECESITLIH.

Elsewhere in Central America, ORIT and AIFLD have adopted the same techniques to control the activities of trade unions (see box, p.40). But nowhere in Central America have pro-US unions won such a complete grip over the trade union and peasant movement as in Honduras. In El Salvador and Guatemala, thousands of workers grew disillusioned in the 1970s with the conciliatory tactics adopted by

39

The AIFLD and ORIT

AIFLD (American Institute for Free Labor Development)

Formed in 1961 at the suggestion of George Meany, head of AFL-CIO (American Federation of Labor — Congress of International Organisations) for 36 years, AIFLD has been the main vehicle for US labour policy in Latin America and the principal influence on the direction of ORIT. The AIFLD receives some funds from the AFL-CIO, but much the largest share of its budget comes from the US government and corporations, representatives of which are among its directors. Companies giving donations to AIFLD include W.R. Grace, Shell, ITT, Exxon, IBM, United Fruit and 85 others. J. Peters Grace, the first chairman of AIFLD, stated that 'through the AIFLD, business, labour, and government have come together to work toward a common goal in Latin America, namely supporting the democratic form of government, the capitalist system and the general well-being of the individual'. AIFLD has trained over 200,000 Latin American trade unionists, many of them at its 'graduate school' in Virginia. It has frequently been accused of having close associations with the CIA: Philip Agee, former CIA agent and author of 'CIA Diary', described AIFLD as a 'CIA-controlled labour centre financed through AID [with] programmes in adult education and social projects used as a front for covering trade-union organising activity'. Such activities have included training for trade union involvement in the CIA-supported overthrow of Cheddi Jagan in Guyana in 1964, and the right-wing coups in Brazil in 1964 and Chile in 1973.

ORIT (Organización Regional Inter-Americana del Trabajo/Inter-American Regional Organisation of Labor)

ORIT is the American affiliate of the ICFTU (International Confederation of Free Trade Unions). From its foundation in 1951, ORIT has fallen under the influence of the AFL-CIO, and has been a resolute pro-US and anti-communist labour body. ORIT's aim has usually been to further what it calls 'democratic trade unionism', which emphasises the need for labour to stay out of electoral politics and argues that there is a basic harmony between capital and labour. ORIT works closely with the US State Department and labour attaches at US embassies, and has a large number of training scholarships and financial benefits available for member unions.

'official' trade union leaders, and pressed for greater confrontation and radical change. By the end of the 1970s, many unions had identified with the broader popular movement which was giving active support to the armed struggle. In Honduras, although left-wing militants continued to press for more radical trade union action, they have been unable to displace permanently the ORIT bureaucracy from power.

FESITRANH and FECESITLIH became the central axis of the Honduran trade union movement and in 1964 united to form the Confederation of Honduran Workers (CTH), together with the National Association of Peasants (ANACH). Throughout the 1960s and '70s, CTH and ANACH enjoyed much higher levels of membership than rival unions. Given the difficulty of organising separate confederations, the left wing attempted, with limited success, to win the pro-ORIT unions to more radical positions. Communists briefly captured the leadership of FECESITLIH in the 1960s, and although they lost control of the SITRASFRUCO leadership in 1963, they did gain control of SITRATERCO from 1975 until 1981. The combination of anti-communism, selective repression and gangsterism by which the pro-government and pro-ORIT 'democratic front' regained control of SITRATERCO in the 1980s was in essence the same tactic which had been used nearly 30 years before in the 1954 strike. The breaking of that strike had successfully paved the way for a more sophisticated approach to controlling the labour movement than the mass killings and disappearances carried out by neighbouring governments, and had set a clear pattern for Honduran labour relations.

The Military Step In

The beginnings of economic modernisation, the introduction of Gálvez's reforms, and the militancy of the banana workers had all increased political instability in the mid-1950s. Not surprisingly, the traditional political structures were slow to adjust to the more complex array of social forces. It was only following a period of political uncertainty between 1954 and 1957 that constitutional government emerged in the shape of the elected civilian administration of the Liberal, Villeda Morales. Ironically, Villeda's victory at the polls in 1957 was only possible because in the previous year the armed forces had made their first entry onto the Honduran political stage.

Following Gálvez's relatively stable six years in power from 1948 to 1954, Honduras' elites were once again racked by bitter infighting, with no party able to come out firmly on top. When the Liberals won the 1954 elections by a clear majority, they were prevented from taking power by the refusal of the Nationalists and their allies to

41

provide a quorum for the confirmation of the Liberal president. When the Nationalist politician, Julio Lozano Díaz, took over the presidency in 1954, he too could not retain power without resorting to Carías-type repression. He used violence and exile to crush a student strike in 1956 and a short-lived Liberal revolt. Leading Liberals were banished from the country in July of that year, and when Liberal supporters occupied the army barracks in Tegucigalpa, 90 people were killed by government forces.

Neither the Honduran army nor the US government favoured such methods at the time, as they threatened to accentuate political instability. When Lozano attempted to maintain himself in power, in October 1956 a group of military officers launched their first ever *coup d'état* to overthrow him and guarantee the elections of 1957.

Despite their late entry into Honduran politics, over the next 30 years the military were to become the most important political institution in the country. The political stalemate between the two traditional parties in 1956 meant that the army initially acted as caretaker in the power struggle between them. But soon, as the only strong and centralised institution in the country, the army stepped permanently into the political vacuum. The weakness of the Honduran elite, whose political and economic power had been historically eclipsed by the US multinationals, facilitated this process. They were without the resources to support an army that could use its coercive might exclusively on their behalf. The result was that the relationship between the Honduran military and the elites never achieved the level of extensive collaboration shown by their counterparts in El Salvador and Guatemala. Although the traditional political parties, and especially the Nationalists, would ally themselves with the army, the narrow interests of the Honduran elite were not automatically left unchallenged by the military. On a number of occasions, but especially in the early 1970s, sectors of the Honduran army were to demonstrate a degree of political autonomy from the major landowning, business and commercial groups.

The origins of the Honduran army differed in a number of ways from those of its neighbours in Guatemala and El Salvador. In both these countries, the oligarchies, which had emerged with the coffee boom and liberal reforms at the end of the nineteenth century, had created their own professional armies. In Guatemala, the coffee planters had needed an efficient security force to manage the state and maintain public order on their behalf. El Salvador's coffee-growers, by contrast, had maintained direct control of the state until the peasant rebellion of 1932 prompted military intervention under Hernández Martínez, thereby beginning a 50-year period in which the armed forces would control the machinery of state on behalf of the

Sam 'the banana man' Zemurray.   *Tiburcio Carías Andino.*

Oswaldo López Arellano.   *Ramón Villeda Morales.*

oligarchy. In both countries the army identified closely with the oligarchy, and did not seriously challenge their economic and political interests.

In Honduras the situation was different. A strong, centralised state had not emerged in the nineteenth century. There was no expulsion of peasants from communal lands, and in contrast to El Salvador and Guatamala, an armed force had not been required to repress the resistance to this process or to force peasants to work on the coffee plantations. Early efforts to forge a national army had been made by rival elites, but they had floundered amid the political infighting which characterised Honduran politics until 1929. Even under Carías, the armed forces remained a weak, unprofessional force. Regional military commanders enjoyed considerable local autonomy, as did the private police corps of the fruit companies in the banana enclaves. Until the 1950s, military officers continued to think of themselves as attached to particular regional leaders, rather than as members of a professional military institution.

Nevertheless, Carías had begun efforts to professionalise and modernise the army, and in particular the air force. This process gathered pace after 1948 with considerable support and guidance from the US. At the beginning of the 1940s, Carías had set up the country's first officer training school, which in 1952, under the direction of US officers, was converted into the Francisco Morazán Military Academy. This in effect marked the foundation of the Honduran professional army. The close relationship with the US was cemented by the military treaty signed on 25 May 1954, the terms of which resembled the 1903 pact in which the United States had made a virtual colony out of Panama. The basic deal was that the US promised military aid in return for unlimited access to Honduran raw and semi-processed materials in the event of deficiencies in its own resources. With US help, military schools were set up, scholarships granted, and modern military equipment supplied. For the first time, army bases were established on a national basis, which hastened the decline of the regional commanders. The army had become a professional institution, with a sense of its own political power and independence from the civilian elites.

There was one more important change in the army's structure. Until 1957 the armed forces had been directly dependent on the elected civilian executive. The new constitution of that year, engineered by the outgoing defence minister, Lt.-Col. Oscar López Arellano (later to become president) changed this relationship. From 1957 onwards, the chief of the armed forces — nominated by the high command — had ultimate control over the institution, which became formally independent of any elected government. An elected president could appoint a defence minister, but his power and responsibilities would be much reduced. But most significantly, the military wrote into the constitution the right of the head of the armed forces to disobey presidential orders it considered unconstitutional.

The coup of 1963 against the Liberal administration of Villeda Morales marked the emergence of the Honduran army as an independent political force, with enough confidence to seize government for themselves. Even during the interim civilian government of Ramón Ernesto Cruz in 1971 and the Suazo Córdova administration post-1981, the Honduran army was to remain the most important political actor in the country for the next 20 years. Its historical development had given it two essential characteristics. First, it was more susceptible to US influence than its counterparts elsewhere in the region; secondly, unlike the Guatemalan and Salvadorean armies, who held power only through repression, sectors of the Honduran military would experiment with different political alliances which at times included peasant and labour unions. Although the objective was to co-opt and control these movements, it was a style of political behaviour which occasionally distinguished the Honduran armed forces from its neighbours.

4 The Limits to Reform

Honduras and the Central American Crisis: A Background

Until the 1980s, Honduras was largely immune from the political turmoil affecting the neighbouring countries of El Salvador, Nicaragua and Guatemala. Yet Honduras shares many of the problems at the root of the Central American crisis. Most Hondurans are still desperately poor, and poorer than their neighbours. In 1979, *per capita* income was US$480 dollars, nearly 50 per cent lower than that of Nicaragua, the second poorest country in Central America. Since 1963, Honduras has been ruled almost continuously by a series of corrupt military rulers, as is the norm throughout the region, except for Costa Rica, and after 1979, Nicaragua. Honduras also shares the grossly unequal system of land tenure characteristic of its neighbours (see diagram, p.47). A comparison between the agrarian censuses in El Salvador and Honduras in the early 1970s showed that in both countries two per cent of the farms covered nearly one-half of the land, while two-thirds of the farms were squeezed into ten per cent of the land area. In addition, lower levels of land fertility in Honduras suggested that smallholders were worse off than their Salvadorean counterparts as they needed more land to survive.

But despite these characteristics, by 1980 Honduras had not spawned guerrilla organisations comparable to the FMLN in El Salvador, the Sandinistas in Nicaragua, or the URNG in Guatemala. This chapter draws out some of the distinct features of Honduran social and political developments in the 1960s and '70s, which help explain both why Honduras is poorer but politically more stable than its neighbours, and why the US was able to turn Honduras into the 'Pentagon Republic' in the 1980s.

The Honduran economy of the 1950s was still largely agrarian.

Land Distribution by Farm Size in Honduras, 1974

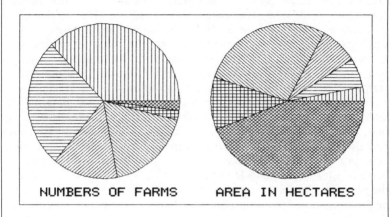

NUMBERS OF FARMS   AREA IN HECTARES

Farm size in hectares*	No. of farms	%	No. of hectares	%	Key
Under 2	72,421	37	75,100	3	▯
2-5	52,360	27	163,803	6	▤
5-10	28,264	14	201,274	8	▨
10-50	34,390	18	729,361	28	◩
50-100	4,433	2	301,228	11	▦
More than 100	3,473	2	1,160,003	44	▨
Total	195,341	100	2,630,859	100	

*1 hectare = 2.47 acres.

Notes:
1. This data only refers to privately-owned land.
2. The figures only report the distribution of farm holdings — as major landowners typically own more than one farm, land distribution is even more unequal.
3. In 1974, there were 108,621 landless rural families, who made up 36% of the rural population. Assuming farms of less than 2 hectares are insufficient to support a peasant family adequately, the landless and land poor encompass 60% of the rural population.

Source: Third Agrarian Census, 1974.

Eighty-one per cent of the economically active population worked in agriculture, 85 per cent of the population lived in the countryside, and over 40 per cent of GDP was provided by the agricultural sector. The takeover of large areas of northern Honduras by the banana companies in the early twentieth century had not affected the social structure of the country as a whole. The companies employed a very small percentage of the workforce and the areas in which they operated tended to be inaccessible, underpopulated and ridden with malaria. Although the 1952 census revealed that the top 4 per cent of farms covered 57 per cent of the territory and the smallest 65 per cent only 15 per cent, friction between peasants and paternalistic landowners was rare. However, starting in the mid-1950s and early '60s, pressure on the land built up as landowners took over more land and diversified into new export crops as a result of the incentives inaugurated under President Gálvez. An increasing number of Salvadoreans migrated to Honduras at this time in search of land, and the fruit companies began to sack large numbers of workers. Strong peasant organisations soon began to challenge the major landowners. They put increasing pressure on successive governments to give them land or settle land disputes in their favour. But when the pressure on the land grew, Honduran governments were able to implement the agrarian reforms of 1962, 1972 and 1975, which, although severely limited in their achievements, absorbed some of the peasants' demands and prevented a major social explosion.

The implementation of even this limited agrarian reform distinguishes Honduras from its neighbours. The constant battle between the landless and land-poor and large landowners is pivotal to the course of events elsewhere in the region. The political and social breakdown affecting Guatemala, El Salvador and Nicaragua stemmed not from economic stagnation (GDP growth over the two decades was high by international standards), but from the social effects of diversification into new export crops, particularly cotton and sugar. The larger estates took over more and more land for export production, evicting peasants who had previously worked it and forcing them onto more marginal lands or to migrate to urban areas in search of jobs. The effects of diversification were particularly acute in El Salvador because of the narrow limits on land availability; 12 per cent of the rural population were without land in 1961, and by 1975 this figure had risen to 40 per cent.

Honduras adopted a similar agro-export model, but here the effects were less catastrophic. There was less demographic pressure on the land than in El Salvador, which was seven times as densely populated as Honduras in 1961. Even though this ratio drops if Honduras' higher percentage of mountainous areas is taken into account,

Honduras possesses large unused lands potentially suitable for cultivation and colonisation given appropriate infrastructural development. But more significant than population density was the availability of state-owned land which successive governments could distribute to peasants who had become displaced or landless. As described in chapter 2, after Independence large amounts of public and *ejido* land were not abolished in order to make way for coffee production. The failure of the liberal reforms at the end of the nineteenth century meant that as late as 1952, only 48 per cent of the national territory was held as private property, while 52 per cent was either nationally-owned or *ejido* land. This in turn meant that in the 1960s and '70s Honduran governments could avoid antagonising the landed oligarchy by distributing state-owned, and not privately-owned land. In fact, by 1980, of the 200,000 hectares handed out to peasant families, only one-fifth was private property that had been expropriated or bought, whereas the remaining 81 per cent was national land. In El Salvador and Guatemala, it was impossible to have an agrarian reform without confronting the landed oligarchy.

An important characteristic of the agrarian reform process in Honduras was that it encouraged the formation of production and service cooperatives which were able to coexist with, and even complement, existing forms of land tenure. In fact, the major capitalist landowners, and especially the fruit companies, were able to transfer the costs and risks of production onto small peasant co-operatives created by the agrarian reform. In exchange for technical and financial assistance provided by the Agrarian Reform Institute or the companies, these cooperatives began to grow export crops, while the multinationals kept control of the most profitable areas such as marketing and distribution.

One of the main political dimensions to the Central American conflagration is the refusal of elites — the military and oligarchies in El Salvador and Guatemala, and Somoza in Nicaragua — to accept any political reforms or liberalisation. In both El Salvador and Guatemala, the army intervened openly to prevent electoral victories by opposition parties in the 1970s, while in Nicaragua President Somoza manipulated each election in his favour. In Honduras, however, limited reform was a political option. Since no strong cohesive coffee oligarchy had developed in the nineteenth century, the nation's largest domestic landowners continued to be technologically backward cattle-raisers as late as 1950. They constituted the economically poorest and politically weakest rural oligarchy in Central America. Against this background, the Honduran military enjoyed more autonomy from the traditional elites than their Central American counterparts, and were prepared to form political alliances with industrialists and peasant and trade union organisations. The economic weakness of the Honduran elites was matched by the political ineptitude of the Liberal and National Parties, which traditionally represented them. Both parties (but especially the Nationalists) tried to ally themselves with the army as their only means of regaining access to the state's resources.

However, by 1980 the limits on the reform process had become all too apparent. The three agrarian reforms reflected primarily the political objectives of Honduran politicians and the military, in particular the need to control and co-opt the peasant movement rather than the will to tackle the basic economic and social problems of the country. Honduran elites remained deeply corrupt and ready to plunder the state's resources for private gain. Attempts to modernise and industrialise the economy were mostly thwarted by this basic characteristic of those who ran the state, and the country was condemned to a series of weak leaders prepared to mortgage their country's sovereignty and future.

Ramón Villeda, 1957-1963: The First Attempt at Reform

The new Liberal president of 1957, Ramón Villeda Morales, declared that Honduras was 'the country of the seventies — 70 per cent illiteracy, 70 per cent illegitimacy, 70 per cent rural population, and 70 per cent avoidable deaths'. Backed by the new urban middle class and sectors of the organised working class, his Liberal administration heralded the start of 15 years of moderate reforms aimed at easing rural tensions and modernising the economy. After the success of the Cuban revolution in 1959, Villeda was also supported by the Kennedy administration in the US, who pushed for social reform as a means of preempting more revolutions. Villeda's anti-communism and acute sensitivity to private enterprise and property dovetailed neatly with US proposals for change through the Alliance for Progress. However, Villeda's reforms were considered too radical by the fruit companies and the landed oligarchy, who together with conservative allies in the army conspired against his regime and eventually secured its overthrow in 1963.

Villeda's economic policy carried on from where the Gálvez and Lozano administrations had left off. It was designed to expand the internal market and reduce dependence on the imports of manufactured goods. Various incentives were introduced to stimulate industrial development, and in 1961 Honduras joined the Central American Common Market (CACM). The CACM was an attempt to

Settlers of the Nueva Concepción colonisation plan.

51

promote the industrialisation of the Central American economies through reducing trade barriers between member states, opening up regional markets for local industries and protecting them against more advanced competitors with a common external tariff system. However, it was not long before the Honduran industrialisation plan resulted in a further penetration of US capital and increased US control of the economy.

In the social area, a national welfare board was set up, the education budget doubled with the support of substantial loans from USAID, and the country's first labour law of 1959 established legal trade union organisation along the lines recommended by the now dominant ORIT and AFL-CIO.

However, it was in the rural areas, and especially on the northern coast, where Villeda had to face the most pressure for reforms. The infrastructural backup, credit support and technical assistance given to the promotion of new export crops after the second world war had begun to have profound effects on the Honduran agrarian structure and the availability of land. Coffee, beef and cotton became important exports for the first time during the 1950s and '60s, while bananas, which had contributed 88 per cent of the value of Honduran exports in the 1925-39 period, declined to 45 per cent by 1960. Cotton plantations increased from 1,200 hectares in 1950 to 18,200 hectares in 1965, creating intense land pressure in the cotton zones of Choluteca and other parts of southern Honduras where population density was most acute. The amount of land given over to cattle-raising (mostly in the north) expanded by 300,000 hectares between 1952 and 1965 to accommodate an increase in the number of cattle from 431,000 to 719,000. Coffee production, too, more than doubled between 1945 and 1960.

However, coffee tended to be grown on small and medium-sized farms (although its marketing was monopolised by a few exporters). The modernised cattle ranches, on the other hand, and the new cotton plantations were large-scale commercial enterprises, which took over thousands of acres of public and *ejido* land by simply evicting tenants and squatters and erecting barbed wire fences around the land they wanted. Peasants who managed to find new land to rent suddenly discovered that rents had shot up to match the rise in land value. The changes in land use coincided with an increase in the population growth rate, the arrival of Salvadorean migrants and the sacking of the banana workers, thereby putting pressure on the land for the first time in the country's history.

From the mid-1950s onwards, a growing number of conflicts developed between landowners and displaced peasants around the legality of possession, the encroachment of commercial farms onto

52

peasant lands, and the traditional landowners' practice of leaving large areas of their land idle. As it was no longer so easy as before for peasants to move to new land, they began to resist the landowners with increasing militancy and organisation. In particular, the ex-banana workers, who had gained considerable union experience on the plantations, began organising Honduras' first national peasant union in the late 1950s. Finally constituted in August 1962, the National Federation of Honduran Peasants (FENACH) concentrated its efforts on mobilising renters and sharecroppers on land where United Fruit was trying to expand its cattle-raising operations.

On assuming power, Villeda was immediately petitioned by peasant groups to adjudicate in their favour and guarantee their access to land. The government initiated a major programme of agricultural colonisation, distributing some 75,000 acres of national and *ejido* land in areas of low population density. In 1961 Villeda established the National Agrarian Institute (INA) to oversee the process. A year later, in September 1962, he sponsored a new pro-US peasant union, the National Association of Honduran Peasants (ANACH). Like its urban counterparts, ANACH enjoyed extensive ORIT support, and was set up to challenge what the government believed was communist influence in FENACH.

Villeda's most significant measure was a major piece of legislation designed to challenge the right of the landlords to leave their land unfarmed. The 1962 agrarian reform had three main aims: first to bring into production idle or poorly utilised lands and make the old landowners more efficient; secondly to create a legal basis for the recuperation of public and *ejido* land, which the fruit companies and landowners had illegally occupied; and thirdly to absorb some of the *campesino* pressure by giving land to peasants in individual plots.

Despite the mildness of its aims, the reform gave rise to bitter objections both from the fruit companies and from local landowning interests even before the law had been passed. Although it fitted the policy recommendations of the Alliance for Progress by guaranteeing private property (it set no limit on private property that was adequately utilised), the fruit companies, and particularly United, were threatened by the expropriation of their thousands of acres of uncultivated land. United's opposition prompted the intervention of Charles Burrows, the US ambassador in Tegucigalpa, who quickly told Villeda not to allow the law to be passed until the State Department had given its approval. In fact, Villeda did sign the legislation, but when United Fruit stopped expanding its operations, he travelled to Miami where he worked out a new version of the bill with the fruit company. In its amended form, the law made it virtually impossible to expropriate private land. As one observer remarked,

'United Fruit had forced the Honduran president to retreat after the US ambassador had failed.'

The campaign against the land reform seriously undermined Villeda's government, but his principal mistake was to alienate the armed forces by trying to keep a paramilitary force independent of their control. Because of its close links to the National Party, the police force was the focus for sectarian conspiracies against Villeda. In response, Villeda had disbanded the police force in 1959 and replaced it with a civil guard dependent on civilian authority. But the army command saw this both as a direct attack on the integrity of the armed forces and an attempt by Villeda to use the civil guard as his own political instrument. Facing a Liberal victory in the 1963 elections, the army moved in, slaughtering many of the civil guard and naming the army commander, Oswaldo López Arellano, as the new president. Although the US broke off relations with Honduras, complaining that 'dictatorships are the seedbeds from which communism ultimately springs up', within six months they had little choice but to recognise the armed forces — their own creation — as the most powerful political institution in the country.

López Arellano, Mark 1, 1963-1971

Although López came to power with the support of right-wing forces who wanted to roll back the mild reforms started under Villeda, he turned out to be a political chameleon. Over the next twelve years, he would act first as a conservative ally of the National Party — as in 1965, when he was 'constitutionally elected' as the Nationalist candidate in blatantly fixed elections — then as a cautious reformist in the late 1960s, and later in 1972 as the champion of the more progressive sectors of the industrial bourgeoisie. But in 1963, the symbol of the early stages of his regime was, according to the US ambassador at the time, 'the president of Standard Fruit and the vice-president of United Fruit sitting in the places of honour during the presidential oath, while foreign dignitaries settled for the less prestigious seats'.

López's first acts were to put an immediate halt to Villeda's social reforms and to repress the most militant sectors of the popular movement. The leaders of both FENACH and the Standard Fruit Workers' Union (SITRASFRUCO), the two main centres of independent trade union activity, were imprisoned and their offices destroyed. Villeda and other Liberal leaders were sent into exile. The Liberals remained weak and divided in their opposition to the marriage of convenience between López and the Nationalists. But López's economic and social policy remained broadly similar to Villeda's. Development efforts centred on the modernisation of the Honduran economy and the integration of Honduras into the CACM, and although the agrarian reform ground to a halt in the first period of his rule, López resurrected the policy later in order to ease rural tension and seek a political base.

The most important plank of López's modernisation plan was the Common Market. Trade and investment increased substantially in the first half of the 1960s, and Honduran industrial production grew at an average of some 11 per cent per year. By the end of the '60s, the industrial sector's contribution to GNP had increased from 12 to 16 per cent. But the growth obscured two major problems. First, US multinationals were the principal beneficiaries of the improved investment climate and expanding markets. Second, as a direct result of US influence, initial plans for development on a regional basis were jettisoned, leading to acute imbalances between the member nations.

Under the market rules, foreign capital was allowed to acquire local firms and dominate new areas of investment. In Honduras, the banana companies, and in particular Standard Fruit, began to expand into the manufacturing sector. They used a local company, the Cervecería de Honduras, as a holding company to control a number of other companies, often with local capital as junior partners. Between 1961 and 1965, US$200 million of private, mostly US, capital, was pumped into the Honduran economy, while total US investment doubled between 1963 and 1967. Of the 63 major companies in Honduras, 35 were founded between 1960 and 1968. Among the top 50, US multinationals controlled 100 per cent of the production of the largest five firms and 89 per cent of the largest 20. The two largest Honduran banks, Banco Atlántida and the Banco de Honduras, came respectively under the control of Chase Manhattan in 1967 and the First National City Bank in 1965. In sum, the CACM did not reduce the control of foreign capital over the Honduran economy, but only extended it into new areas of operation. In addition to the banana industry, the mining companies and the key infrastructure which US firms already owned, they now controlled the banking system and the most important industrial sectors.

Moreover, because of the influence of US companies, member countries paid little attention to maintaining a regional balance between the less developed countries like Honduras and Nicaragua and the stronger, more industrial economies of El Salvador, Guatemala and Costa Rica. The mechanism by which industrial development should have been coordinated, the integrated industries plan, was quietly forgotten. Capital flooded into El Salvador and

Guatemala at a much greater rate than into Honduras, and the competitive gap between Honduras and its neighbours widened. In 1960 Honduran industrial GNP was 51 per cent of El Salvador's — by 1969 it had dropped to 32.5 per cent. Between 1960 and 1968, Salvadorean exports to Honduras had increased fivefold, whereas Honduran sales to El Salvador had only doubled. With protective barriers removed, Honduran manufacturers were forced out of business as cheap Salvadorean and Guatemalan products swamped the local market.

By the late 1960s, trade deficits, unemployment and corruption were all increasing. Since much of the investment through CACM was capital-intensive, few jobs were created. Unemployment rose by 25 per cent between 1961 and 1967. In addition, many Honduran businessmen who were keen to take advantage of the new opportunities opened up by CACM, were hamstrung by the appalling corruption and mismanagement of López's National Party government. For example, the Central American Bank for Economic Integration (BCIE) reported in 1967 that a mere 30 per cent of development loans to the Honduran government had actually been disbursed. López found himself losing support among the business community and urban middle classes, but again it was in the rural areas that the real pressure was mounting.

Between 1962 and 1966, only twelve peasant groups had received land under the 1962 agrarian reform law, while the colonisation programmes were collapsing for lack of credit and technical assistance. But the same pressures which had originally given rise to the law built up. Continuing US demands for sugar and beef encouraged the large landowners to expand their operations. Tenancy and share cropping rights were revoked, and peasants were driven off their own or public land to make way for the increase in land given over to pasture. But the peasant unions were now stronger and better organised. Following the imprisonment of FENACH leaders and the destruction of their El Progreso based offices in 1963, a hard core of FENACH members led by Lorenzo Zelaya had fled to the mountains of Yoro to establish a guerrilla front. Even though they were crushed at El Jute in April 1965, many of FENACH's other members drifted into the parallel union created by Villeda, ANACH, radicalising it. In the southern departments of Valle and Choluteca, various peasant communities banded together in 1964 to form ACASCH (the Social-Christian Peasant Association of Honduras). ACASCH was a direct product of the pastoral work of the Catholic Church, which during the 1950s had established a series of community development programmes, such as radio schools, consumer cooperatives, women's and youth clubs and local public work projects, many of which were

56

Testimony of Marcial Caballero, Head of the National Union of Peasants (UNC)

I was born in a small town in northern Honduras, La Mora. We were ten children in the family. My father worked for the United Fruit Company for 30 years. He devoted his entire life to the company, never missing a day's work. But when he started to get old and tired, the company gave him a few dollars and forced him to retire.

Homeless, we went to live on a piece of land abandoned by the company. It was bad land but we cleared it and managed to get by, growing rice, beans and corn, and hunting animals.

One day, after we had been living there for two years, someone from the company came and told us we had eight days to leave. The big landowners did that all the time. They would let the peasants take over some of the land they weren't using, wait until they had done the backbreaking work clearing the land, and then kick them out.

Well, three days after they had come to warn us, they returned with soldiers. The soldiers burned our house down, beat my father, and took him off to jail. He was so badly beaten that when he got out of jail, he couldn't work any more and died six months later.

I was the oldest son, and I was soon drafted into the army for three years. When I got home, I found my family living by the side of the road. A company called Citrus Export had come to claim the land. It wasn't just my family, but 65 families in the area were all evicted from land they had been living on for years.

My mother was sick and thin as a rail, my brothers and sisters were starving. There were no jobs around. There was no land to farm. The neighbours' children were also dying of hunger and the people were desperate. I went with some of the other peasants to discuss our situation with the local priest, and he told us how elsewhere in the country peasants were organising to fight for their rights. He also told us about a government reform institute, INA, that was supposed to help landless peasants. I was delegated to go to the capital and ask INA for help.

We took a collection for the trip, but the money was only enough for the bus fare. I spent three days there without a cent, sleeping outside and going hungry. Every day I would get up at dawn and be the first one there. I would watch people going in and out all day, but they kept me sitting there and at the end of the day would say, 'Sorry, no time today. Maybe tomorrow.' I didn't want to disappoint the others, they had put so much faith in me. But after three days I realised that nobody wanted to talk to a poor peasant like me, so I went back home.

When I got home, all the neighbours were waiting. They were so mad at the way I'd been treated. The next week, at three o'clock in the morning, we moved back onto the land. By 10 o'clock the same day, we were greeted by the company manager, 60 soldiers . . . and a representative from INA.

The guy from INA tried to reason with us. 'Look, you can't just take over the land like that. First you've got to file a request at INA, with the names and identification of all the families, their birth certificates, etc. Then INA will investigate the problem. They'll do a socioeconomic study of all the families. Then they'll survey the land. Then they'll pass on the information from the municipality to the national level. And if they think the claim is valid, it will get passed on to INA's board to make the final decision.' Our heads were spinning. We realised it would take years to do all that, and what were we to do in the meantime? Starve? Besides, it was our land. All we were doing was 'recovering' what was ours to begin with.

But we didn't want to get shot either. So we left the land and came back after the soldiers had left. [A few weeks later] the company manager, Mr Smith, showed up with six armed men and started to threaten us. 'Get out of here today, you filthy peasants, or I'll use your blood as fertiliser,' he shouted. So we held up our rifles and machetes and replied, 'OK, if that's the way you want it. But it won't be our blood alone.'

He turned around and saw all the peasants behind him with their rifles and machetes and changed his tune. 'Calm down, boys,' he said. 'I was only kidding. I'm sure we can work something out to our mutual benefit.' We took their guns away from them and let them go.

A few days later, I was home eating dinner when a group of men came to my house. We had called on one of the peasant unions for help, and I thought these men were from the unions. But when I got up to shake their hands, they pulled out their guns, beat me, and dragged me off to jail.

The next day the manager came to see me. 'You're a young, bright guy,' he told me. 'Why get yourself into trouble over these dumb peasants?' And he offered me a good job with lots of money so my family could live decently. 'Look,' I told the manager, 'it's not just my family I'm concerned about but the others as well. Why don't you just let us have that land? For you that little piece of land is nothing. For us it's the difference between life and death.'

When he left, the torture began and lasted for a week. They tried to get me to sign a paper saying the land belonged to the company, but I refused. So they finally told me I'd be shot by firing squad. They tied me to a tree, blindfolded me and fired. The shots rang out in the air and I could hear them laughing hysterically. 'You can go home now,' they said, 'But remember, if you make the slightest noise, we'll not only get you, but your whole family.'

What they didn't understand is that their efforts only made us more determined. We took over the land again, but this time we held on to it. And I went to work for the UNC, so I could help other poor people fight for their rights.

Source: Honduras Update, March 1985.

---

later taken over by the Christian Democrats. But from 1965 onwards, ACASCH turned its attention to recovering lost land and demanding more access to land, a change in orientation which brought it into increasing conflict with local farmers.

Conservative landowners reacted to the peasant resistance and takeover of idle lands by forming their own organisation. In 1966, a group of cattle ranchers united to set up the National Federation of Honduran Farmers and Cattle-raisers (FENAGH), which spear-headed opposition to peasant land seizures and put pressure on the government to resolve land disputes in their favour. For the first time, Honduras was seeing the rise of a cohesive landowning elite which had much in common with the traditional rural oligarchies of Guatemala and El Salvador. The difference was that the Honduran military was not their automatic ally.

Early in 1967, with land occupations increasing, López revitalised the agrarian reform, as part of his own search for a new political base. After ANACH threatened to stage a hunger march on the capital, López met with their leaders, and as a result committed new financial support to INA and appointed a new, more active director, Rigoberto Sandoval Corea. Although Sandoval gave INA a more 'pro-peasant' stance, much of its effectiveness was limited by the greater economic and legal resources available to the large landowners in any disputes. The reaction of FENAGH was predictable — INA officials were labelled as 'enemies of private property'.

INA also changed the nature of its aims. It now promoted cooperatives, the model of which was the Guanchías cooperative. Guanchías was begun in 1965 on land returned to the government by United Fruit. Initially, it produced corn for sale on the local market, but on the basis of credits from INA and the National Development Bank it soon expanded, and in 1968 planted 500 acres of bananas which it then sold to Standard Fruit. Guanchías' success led to other peasant groups adopting a cooperative structure. INA made co-operative assistance and training a cornerstone of its agrarian reform programme, and in turn the national peasant organisations were strengthened by INA's insistence that reform beneficiaries be organised into production co-ops. However, the success of the arrangement with Guanchías opened the eyes of Standard and United to ways of using the agrarian reform to their own advantage. López's first period in office had shown that peasant demands for land could be partially met without alienating the agro-commercial interests of the fruit companies or the cattle ranchers. As Stephen Volk of the North American Congress on Latin America (NACLA) observed, 'in neighboring El Salvador, this equation would have been utterly contradictory and virtually unthinkable'.

The Football War

Despite the revitalisation of the agrarian reform, the continued weakness of Honduran industry and the growth of cash crop production reinforced basic social conflicts and regional tensions. The so-called 'football war' of 1969 between El Salvador and Honduras had very little to do with football. In fact, it sprang from the growing tensions over land within each country and the trade imbalance within the CACM.

While Honduran manufacturers were still suffering from Salvadorean competition (in the first six months of 1969, the Honduran trade deficit with El Salvador was US$5 million), thousands of Salvadoreans were becoming caught up in the battles between FENAGH and the peasant movement. Since the 1900s, when the banana companies had brought thousands of labourers from El Salvador to settle and work on the banana plantations, Salvadoreans had formed a permanent minority in Honduras. By the end of the 1960s, some 300,000 had filtered through the porous borders separating the two countries. They constituted around 20 per cent of Honduras' rural population and owned over 200,000 acres of national land. As many as half of them had arrived after the boom in commercial agriculture in the 1950s and '60s.

The cattle ranchers of FENAGH started to blame the Salvadoreans for the lack of land, in a crude attempt to divert attention from what was essentially an internal conflict. They won willing support from the ranks of the National Party, and its 'Mancha Brava' goon squads began to harass the Salvadorean migrants. López was happy to go along with FENAGH's campaign. By escalating the tension with El Salvador, he could channel increasing social discontent away from his regime. INA too caught the mood. In May 1969, they gave a group of 57 Salvadorean families 30 days to 'return their land' to the Honduran state, and one month later evicted some 500 Salvadorean settlers. Thousands of the migrants began to return to El Salvador, some of them with stories of beatings and harassment. For the Salvadorean government, it was not just a question of national pride — they were greatly concerned by the social consequences for El Salvador of the returning migrants.

It was within this context that in June 1969 the two countries met to determine who should represent the Central America and Caribbean region in the 1970 World Cup. At the game in Tegucigalpa (which Honduras won), the Salvadorean press speculated about the possible poisoning of their team's food. At the game in San Salvador (which Honduras lost), Salvadoreans attacked visiting Honduran supporters with fireworks. In response, Honduras expelled thousands more Salvadoreans from its countryside, prompting the Salvadorean government to seal its borders, and to file a complaint of 'genocide' with the Inter-American Human Rights Commission. Early in July, Salvadorean troops crossed into Honduran territory to 'defend the human rights of their countrymen'.

The war lasted one hundred hours. Although the Honduran air force scored one notable success when its pilots destroyed El Salvador's oil refinery at Acajutla, only the intervention of the Organisation of American States (OAS) saved its ill-organised and corruption-ridden army from defeat. El Salvador's more professional and better-trained troops advanced deep into Honduran territory before the OAS threatened an economic boycott.

The war had a number of important long-term consequences for Honduras. First, it left a simmering border dispute which disrupted (and continues to disrupt) relations between the two countries. Secondly, the withdrawal of Honduras from the CACM heralded its effective demise, and opened the way for the new industrialisation plans of the 1970s. Thirdly, the ignomonious defeat of the Honduran army highlighted its inefficient and corrupt command structure, and thereby strengthened the hand of younger and more professional soldiers. Many of these younger officers were to be a major force

61

behind López's reforms in the early 1970s.

When large-scale land invasions intensified after the war, it became even more apparent that the Salvadorean migration had not been the cause of the rural crisis. From 1969 to 1971, INA responded more favourably to peasant occupations, and both the moderate US-backed ANACH and the more radical UNC (which had grown out of ACASCH) grew rapidly in size and influence. With INA's support, other peasant groups formed cooperatives and set up FECORAH (the Federation of Agrarian Reform Cooperatives) in 1970.

A new sense of national unity was also moulded after the war. López, like all the military, had suffered a serious blow to his prestige. He now threw his weight behind the main reformist coalition between the Honduran Confederation of Workers (CTH) and Confederation of Honduran Private Business (COHEP). CTH was made up of the moderate union and peasant federations like ANACH, FECESITLIH and FESITRANH, while COHEP was the Honduran private sector association which tended to represent the small industrial sector around San Pedro Sula, Honduras' second largest city. In order to avoid the rampant sectarianism and corruption which would have inevitably accompanied the return to government by either of the traditional parties, COHEP and the CTH proposed a 'pact of national unity', in which a single, non-partisan candidate would run for president. But the Liberals and Nationalists held out for party elections in which the winning party would be given the presidency and a one-seat majority in Congress. The Nationalist, Ramón Ernesto Cruz, proceeded to win the elections of January 1971, but any hope that the plan might work were soon dispelled.

For a start, as the two parties divided up the top administrative posts, corruption reached new heights. But more significant was the abrupt change in the course of the agrarian reform. Sandoval Corea was replaced at INA by Horacio Moya Posas, a conservative with landowning connections. Far from legalising peasant actions, INA now began to conspire with local landlords and the military to imprison peasant organisers. In the most notorious incident, six peasants from the UNC were assassinated at La Talanquera in Olancho on 18 February 1972 when they refused to abandon an invasion site. The peasants' frustration reached breaking point in December 1972. As thousands joined a major hunger march on Tegucigalpa to demand the application of the agrarian reform law, López launched his second military coup. This time, his support was not the National Party, but an alliance between modernising industrialists and reformist sectors of the popular movement, and a group of younger officers tired of the corruption of civilian politicians.

López Arellano, Mark 2, 1972-1975

If the rhetoric which accompanied the formation of López Arellano's new government was to be believed, Honduras was set for a radical experiment in social and economic reform. But López's promise 'to seize the banners of the left and make the revolution peacefully' soon proved empty in the face of mild opposition from the Honduran right. The young military officers who had pushed López to the left aimed to preempt the possibility of revolutionary upheaval, following the example of the Peruvian military reformist government of 1968. They hoped that by adopting a number of anti-oligarchic and pro-capitalist economic measures, they could promote economic development and hence reduce the social grievances on which the left could feed. But, like the Velasco regime in Peru, they completely failed to develop the necessary social base for their programme. When the right, particularly FENAGH and the fruit companies, counterattacked in 1974, the top-down, state-sponsored programmes of reform had created no popular defence of the regime. As a result, López and his supporters soon lost their way amid a tragi-comedy of incompetence and corruption.

The two pillars of López's regime were a state-sponsored industrialisation plan and agrarian reform. Recognising the failure of the CACM model, López's ministers slowly set in motion a National Development Plan, in which import substitution was again the basic framework but where the state would take a major responsibility for capital investment and accumulation. A series of decrees established state companies and agencies such as COHDEFOR, which reduced the amount of forest lands owned by foreign companies and controlled the production and export of wood products; CONADI, which provided finance for industrial development; and BANASUPO, which bought and sold basic grains. In addition, López got rid of the 'voluntary' contributions paid by civil servants to the traditional political parties, and introduced a minimum wage and a number of other minor social reforms.

However, it was again agrarian reform which was to be the 'fundamental task' of the new regime. Introduced in two stages in 1972 and 1975, the reforms aimed to channel and control the peasant militancy which had brought López to power and, as with the original 1962 law, to raise productivity by bringing into use more under-utilised land owned both by the oligarchy and the state. The interim 1972 decree law no.8 conceded to peasants the temporary right to occupy national and *ejido* land in INA's possession, and obliged private landowners either to rent or cultivate unused land. Decree law no.170 of 1975 extended to 500 hectares the range of private land

Land Distribution under the Honduran Agrarian Reform, 1962-1981

Year(s)	No. of peasant groups	%	No. of families	%	Land distributed in hectares	
1962-66	12	1	453	1	1,357	1
Average (p.a.)	2		91		271	
1967-71	63	5	5,292	10	24,019	10
Average (p.a.)	13		1,058		4,404	
1972	72		3,331		10,585	
1973	224		8,674		32,454	
1974	287		9,828		47,098	
1975	186		6,751		37,252	
1976	182		6,274		26,913	
Total	951	73	34,858	65	154,302	67
1977	106		3,381		15,985	
1978	42		1,745		5,415	
1979	43		1,161		6,355	
1980	63		2,935		9,648	
1981	30		3,981		13,958	
Total	284	22	13,203	25	51,361	22
TOTAL	1,310	101*	53,806	101*	231,039	100

*Due to rounding up.

Note: Yearly averages for the 1972-76 period are 190 groups, 6,972 families, and 30,860 hectares, and for the 1977-81 period, 57 groups, 2,641 families and 10,272 hectares.

Sources: Honduras Update and the International Labour Office.

liable to expropriation, depending on the type of crop, location and soil quality. In broad terms, the laws were directed at breaking up the low-productivity *latifundio/minifundio* system and replacing it with a system of technically efficient and capital-intensive medium- and large-sized farms on the one hand, and labour-intensive cooperatives on the other. The framework of the reform was always anti-oligarchic, and never anti-capitalist.

1972-1976 were certainly the dynamic years of the agrarian reform.

Workers at the United Fruit processing plant.

By 1976, some 950 peasant groups, representing nearly 35,000 families and covering 154,000 hectares, had benefited (see chart, p.64). These figures represented around 70 per cent of the total beneficiaries and total amount of land distributed for the whole of the 20-year period from 1962 to 1981. Peasant community enterprises were supported by training and back-up supplied by the Peasant Management Project for Agrarian Reform (PROCCARA), a UN-supported outreach programme directed by the Brazilian Clodomir Santos de Morais and staffed by a number of radical agronomists.

It is undeniable that a significant number of peasant groups benefited from the reforms. However, the fundamental political goal of the agrarian reform was to accommodate and control peasant demands for land. While the two reforms clearly acted as a major safety-valve in defusing peasant unrest, independent peasant mobilisation was usually discouraged. Peasant unions and groups which took direct action, usually in the form of land invasions, were excluded from the benefits of the reform. As a result, the reform was top-down, state-sponsored and unresponsive to peasant needs. The reform lacked the genuine participation of the peasants, which could have acted as a stimulus and guarantee of the radicalisation of the process to meet their demands.

Although the peasant unions had 90,000 members by the 1970s, the much less numerous, but economically more powerful conservative opposition groups were able to undermine the López regime. By late 1974, the reform process had slowed considerably in the face of concerted opposition from FENAGH, the fruit companies, the traditional political parties and conservative sectors of the army. In 1973 FENAGH and its supporters had won control of COHEP from the reformist business sectors. With the support of the San Pedro Sula daily, *La Prensa,* COHEP headed a virulent propaganda campaign against the government. FENAGH was incensed by the 1975 law, which in theory put its members' property at risk, although in practice hardly any was expropriated. FENAGH's director charged that the reform 'attacked private property, the democratic system, liberty and individuality'. Both the Nationalists and the Liberals joined the offensive and demanded a return to constitutional rule. While the Nationalists had always enjoyed strong links with FENAGH, the Liberals came under the control of the more conservative *rodista* faction of the party, and threw their weight behind the anti-government campaign.

FENAGH's role was most clearly demonstrated in June 1975 at the Los Horcones massacre. As the implementation of decree law 170 was delayed by opposition from the right, the *campesinos* again began to mobilise in protest. In May the UNC sponsored some 100 land occupations in ten different departments, and shortly after, announced five separate marches on Tegucigalpa to force the government to act. In Olancho, a small group of cattle farmers conspired with the local military garrison to stop the march at Juticalpa, 85 miles north of the capital. On 25 June, five of the peasant demonstrators were killed immediately at a UNC training centre, and the bodies of nine others, including two foreign priests from Colombia and the US, were later found at the Los Horcones ranch. According to one report, all nine had been burned to death in bread ovens.

The news of the massacre slowly leaked out. While most Hondurans were shocked by what had happened, the Olancho landowners, according to FENAGH, 'showed themselves the only ones who could respond to the peasant organisations like men'. Although the violent repression of the Horcones massacre was relatively isolated, it succeeded in weakening the UNC and frightening the Honduran church. In the aftermath of Horcones the church moved away from support for radical social change and returned more to charitable responses to the alleviation of poverty.

Company Intervention

The fruit companies and many of their Honduran allies in the armed forces and the San Pedro Sula business community were adopting more subtle methods of controlling the peasant movement than generalised repression. They favoured coopting the movement and channelling the reform to benefit foreign and local capital.

By the mid-1960s, both United and Standard Fruit were changing their commercial strategies in Honduras. Having increased productivity in the 1950s through mechanisation and the adoption of more productive strains of banana, the companies no longer needed so much land. Since their vast, underutilised lands were often the target for peasant occupations, the transfer of some of their land also reduced political risks. Between 1960 and 1975, the two companies reduced their landholdings from 230,000 to 122,000 hectares. Much of the land went to cattle ranchers, but some was sold to independent producers and peasant cooperatives, who continued to grow bananas and other fruit for export which they then sold to the banana companies who continued to control marketing. The companies had grown 87 per cent of Honduran bananas in 1960, but by 1977 the figure had dropped to 60 per cent.

On the basis of the successful experience of the Guanchías cooperative, the companies knew that the arrangement made economic as well as political sense. Because of their monopoly of the world market, the companies could make as much money selling and shipping the bananas as growing them. They could offload costs previously incurred in irrigation, flood control and pesticides onto local producers, and minimise risks from labour disputes or natural disasters (like Hurricane Fifi, which destroyed nearly 60 per cent of agricultural production in September 1974). In the reform sector, the same costs and risks were borne by the Honduran state. In addition, more widespread unionisation since the 1954 strike meant that raising profits by cutting labour could only be achieved at great political cost.

The changing strategy could only work if the companies maintained their control over marketing. But if the reform process was to be deepened, the Honduran state had to get more control over prices and marketing. Two crucial battles were fought against the fruit companies' monopoly. The Bananagate affair and the destruction of the Isletas cooperative showed that the companies were only too prepared to flex their political muscles to maintain their position of privilege.

In the wake of the success of OPEC, during 1974 the world's banana producing countries began discussions which eventually resulted in the establishment of the Union of Banana Exporting Countries (UPEB) and an independent marketing organisation, COMUNBANA. As a preliminary move, the seven governments involved agreed to increase the taxes paid by the fruit companies to the producer countries. United Fruit resorted to its time-honoured policy of bribing government officials. On 3 February 1975, the chairman of United Brands threw himself out of a skyscraper. The resulting investigation into the company's affairs revealed that the company had paid US$1.25 million to a government official (alleged to be López's economy minister, Abraham Bennaton) in exchange for a reversal of an earlier government decision to fix the banana export tax at US$0.50 per crate. Soon after announcing the new tax, the Honduran government had in fact reduced the tax by half, thereby saving United Fruit an estimated US$7.5 million for 1975 alone. When López refused to have his own bank account in Switzerland investigated, he was forced to resign. In the ensuing political crisis, the fruit companies increased their influence over the government. The more conservative Colonel Juan Melgar Castro, who took over from López in April 1975, appointed Guillermo Bueso as president of the Central Bank and César Batres as his political adviser. Bueso enjoyed good contacts with both fruit companies, while Batres was a legal adviser to Standard Fruit.

Despite these links, Melgar Castro was forced to continue the agrarian reform, albeit with a change of emphasis. The Horcones massacre had stimulated further protest from peasant groups. In October 1975 they formed a central front, FUNC (the Peasant Unity Front), consisting of the UNC, ANACH and FECORAH. They issued an ultimatum to Melgar in which they threatened to step up land invasions if there were further delays in the implementation of the reform law. Melgar's response was to launch a lightning land distribution in November 1975, and to reappoint Rigoberto Sandoval Corea as INA's director. But these moves were not as progressive as they first appeared. In 1976, Sandoval's influence was undermined by the formation of a new body, the Agrarian Reform Coordinating Committee, full of powerful landowners who took charge of overall agrarian reform policy. Later in 1977, Melgar Castro unveiled his new agrarian plan whose emphasis was on colonisation projects, especially in the Bajo Aguán river valley on the north coast. It was part of a general move away from land redistribution in favour of land colonisation.

Partly because of the greater representation of the landowners and partly because the colonisation projects tended to be capital-intensive, the speed of the reform slowed to a trickle. Of the 600,000 hectares and 120,000 beneficiaries originally targeted for the period 1975-79, only 15 per cent and 16 per cent respectively were reached (see chart, p.64). According to one estimate, at that rate the original goals would have taken 103 years to achieve.

When Sandoval resigned from INA in 1977, it was widely regarded as closing the last chapter of military reformism. Under the new director, wealthy coffee planter Fabio Salgado, INA's support for the reformed sector sharply deteriorated. Services such as credit, technical assistance and marketing were inadequate and poorly planned, and INA's support for cooperatives and other communal forms of organisation dropped off. Where the leadership of cooperatives began to challenge the companies' monopoly over marketing, INA supported interventions to impose more pliable leaders. The experience of one of the Bajo Aguán cooperatives at Las Isletas (see box, p.70) was a chilling example of how far INA had gone in accommodating the interests of the multinationals.

Corruption and the End of the Reforms

The destruction of Las Isletas was a clear symbol of the military's turn to the right. The reform period finally came to an end in August 1978 when, amid rumours of his involvement in drugs trafficking, Melgar

The Destruction of Las Isletas

In October 1975, the Honduran government established a workers' collective on 2,000 hectares of land abandoned by Standard Fruit after Hurricane Fifi in 1974. An elected board managed the new enterprise, which continued to sell its bananas to Standard. Many of the cooperative's 900 associates had been trade union militants in SUTRASFCO, and as a result, the enterprise was both well-managed and independent. Production increased quickly from 43,000 boxes in 1975 to one million in 1976, and four million the following year. Wages rose from one dollar to three dollars a day. Schools and clinics were set up and women packers were encouraged to join the workers' association. But early in 1977 the cooperative considered selling its bananas to COMUNBANA, the marketing arm of UPEB, instead of Standard Fruit. Secondly, when the company owned the land, the local battalion commander was paid US$4,700 dollars a month as 'compensation for services' — neither he nor any military personnel received anything from the Isletas workers.

Standard and the local army commander connived to change the cooperative's leadership. Backed by troops of the fourth army battalion under the then .Lt.-Col. Gustavo Alvarez (who was on Standard's payroll), a small group of Isletas workers called a special assembly to elect a new leadership. Alvarez's troops arrested 200 members of the cooperative, and guarded the 35 workers who declared themselves to be the new 'democratic' leadership. Economic interests, not 'internal democracy', were behind the move — Standard stood to lose US$2.5 million a year from lost freight charges.

Over the next three years, the new management took Isletas to the brink of bankruptcy by systematically milking the cooperative's capital. Isletas' debt rose from US$4 million in 1977 to US$12 million in 1980. The government banana corporation COHBANA received US$1 million a year from Isletas for 'technical assistance', which in practice, according to the workers, was for '54 sluggards living in air-conditioning . . . and developing an expertise in pool'. Standard of course got its reward: the new leaders signed a long-term contract to market their produce through Standard; they agreed to meet the company's stringent quality standards entailing the use of high-cost fertilisers and pesticides; and they accepted a price per box for their bananas of US$1.46 — US$1.19 less than the price offered by COMUNBANA.

was replaced by a right-wing faction led by General Policarpo Paz García. But the corruption of both the Melgar and Paz governments allowed certain key economic groups and sectors of the army to become very rich by robbing public funds. Although GNP growth, 1976-79, averaged a healthy 7 per cent, the abuse of the state investment agency, CONADI, was a major cause of a doubling of the Honduran debt over the same period.

CONADI had been set up in July 1974 under the López regime in an attempt to develop a national industrial sector. From 1976 to 1978, a total of 67 firms, mostly in the construction and agro-industrial sectors, were supported by loans amounting to 513 million lempiras (US$256.5 million) distributed through CONADI. The small industrial and trading group, largely based in San Pedro Sula, was dominated by families of Arab and Lebanese extraction, who were the descendants of Lebanese Christians who fled to Central America at the turn of the century, to escape Turkish oppression. Representatives of this group, such as the Facussé, Handal and Sikaffy families, borrowed heavily from CONADI, which in turn borrowed heavily on international capital markets where its dealings were underwritten by the Honduran state. Rampant corruption, bad investments and outright theft soon made CONADI effectively bankrupt. By the end of 1981, its debt had risen to nearly 100 million lempiras — of the original 67 firms who had benefited, 58 were in default while only six were responsible for half of CONADI's total debt.

One company, Mejores Alimentos de Honduras owed 20 per cent (19 million lempiras) of the debt. The mother company of Mejores was the financial group Galaxia Comercial e Inversiones, which formed part of the Facussé business emporium. Up until 1976, Mejores was a healthy profit-making company, 89 per cent owned by Galaxia and the rest shared by CONADI and the Central American Bank for Economic Integration. But after 1976, the company made a loss and CONADI took over a major shareholding. In other words, any profits went into private hands while deficits were picked up by CONADI and the Honduran state. But it was the Facussé family who were widely regarded as one of those principally responsible for simply running off with the original CONADI funds. The Honduran state was caught in a vicious circle — the international financial institutions like the IMF and World Bank lent money to the Central Bank so that the Central Bank could pay CONADI what it owed to the foreign banks. As a result, according to one estimate, it had cost CONADI on average 150,000 lempiras to create each new job in the industrial sector. At that rate, it would have needed 58 CONADIs with 30 billion lempiras to find new jobs for the 200,000 unemployed.

The robbing of CONADI was just another example of the capacity of the Honduran elites to use the state's resources for private gain. The scandalous level of corruption throughout the 1960s and '70s contributed to the desperate poverty of the majority of Hondurans. Despite 20 years of reforms, 68 per cent of rural households in 1980 had an income that was insufficient to cover essential consumption, 10 per cent of the population received 50 per cent of the national income, and 5 per cent of the population controlled over half the land. Attempts to industrialise the economy had not broken the iron control of the multinationals — seven of them still controlled 80 per cent of the economy. Of these, Standard and United Fruit were top of the pile. According to the US commercial attache in Tegucigalpa in 1982, 'they had their hands into just about everything in the country' (see appendix 2). Neither they nor the landed oligarchy had been seriously affected by three agrarian reforms. The model of development was still concentrated on boosting agro-export crop production on large commercial farms. According to a 1984 International Labour Office (ILO) study, per capita food production declined by 20 per cent during the 1970s, while agro-export production nearly quadrupled. The Honduran economy was still dominated by the export of just four products — coffee, bananas, meat and timber — which in 1980 accounted for 63 per cent of export earnings, while the marketing of the products was largely controlled by the multinationals.

Despite the partial nature of the reforms, they had clearly contributed to a degree of political stability. In 1980, the beneficiaries of the three agrarian reforms represented 12 per cent of rural families, or 22 per cent of the landless and smallholding population. There had been no equivalent land reform in any other Central American country. Despite the fact that landlessness had increased over the period (according to one estimate, from 1970 to 1980 the number of landless rose some 75,000-110,000 — twice the number of beneficiaries of the agrarian reform between 1962 and 1980), Honduran peasants had at least seen some response from successive governments to their plight. The ability of numerically strong peasant unions to achieve some improvements through syndicalist methods had also defined the nature of their demands, which tended to be localised and often channelled into cooperatives that were not threatening to agro-commercial interests. In addition, the main peasant and trade unions continued to be controlled by the AFL-CIO and ORIT, while their most combative elements were either bought off or repressed. The enormous influence of North American unionism ensured that their demands were channelled through established trade unions and not into independent popular organisations, as in El Salvador or Guatemala, which could offer a sustained challenge to the state. Although militant trade unionists retained considerable influence in some areas, popular support for revolutionary change remained very limited.

The experience of the 1960s and '70s helps to explain why the US found it relatively easy to turn Honduras into the 'Pentagon Republic' in the 1980s. The popular movement was in general weak and co-opted; a corrupt two-party system remained intact and could be resurrected as a facade of democracy; no 'national' industrial groups had emerged capable of staging an independent political or economic project outside the orbit of the multinationals; and within the Honduran army, which was the most important political institution in the country and historically close to the US, the right were firmly in control.

5 Regional Linchpin

Until the middle of 1979, Honduras was never high on the list of priorities for the US government. After the success of the Nicaraguan revolution on 19 July 1979, the Carter administration was quick to identify Honduras as the key ally for containing the revolutionary movements sweeping the region. Just as Carter's decision in April 1980 to increase military aid to the Salvadorean army paved the way for the escalation that followed under Reagan, so Carter also set the agenda for Honduras' new geopolitical role. Honduras' sudden importance to the US government meant that the next five years of Honduran political life would be decisively influenced by the United States and its policy priorities towards the Central American region.

US pressure ensured that elections took place in April 1980 and November 1981 and that the Honduran military allowed a civilian president to take office. The appearance of 'democracy' was essential to US plans for the region. Congress, US public opinion and Latin American and European allies could more easily be rallied behind a policy which involved support for a civilian government, portrayed as a 'fledgling democracy in an oasis of peace' by the US propaganda machine. In fact, at the very point of return to civilian rule in November 1981, US and military control over Honduran political life was strengthened.

Honduras rapidly became the linchpin of US attempts to impose its military solutions on the problems of the Central American region. By 1985, a seemingly endless series of large-scale Honduran and US troop manoeuvres on Honduran soil created the impression that Honduras was an occupied country. In one sense, the massive presence of US troops reflected President Reagan's belief that the Honduran-Nicaraguan frontier is in fact the 'fourth border of the United States'. But they were also reminiscent of the 'big stick' diplomacy of the early twentieth century, when large forces of marines had occupied Cuba,

74

the Dominican Republic and Haiti in the 1920s and '30s, in order to 'protect US property and maintain order' in the face of nationalist opposition. The last extended US occupation of a Central American country had been the attempt to suppress the nationalist rebellion led by the Nicaraguan Augusto Sandino in the 1930s. By a curious twist of history, Sandino's political progeny were threatened 50 years later by the US occupation of neighbouring Honduras.

But this time the US troops were not in Honduras to put down a major internal rebellion; nor was the present set of Honduran leaders bullied into accepting their presence. The US army's public relations officers were at pains to point out that they were the 'invited guests' of the Honduran government. The troops were there because Honduran elites maintained the tradition of subservience to North American interests, providing the rewards were sufficiently attractive. This tradition reached its apogee when the Suazo government suggested to the Kissinger Commission in October 1983 that one future option for Honduras was to become an 'associate state' of the US like Puerto Rico, or a military protectorate like South Korea.

The Carter Project

A mere two months after the Sandinista triumph in Nicaragua, Assistant Secretary of State for Inter-American Affairs, Viron Vaky, presented a major policy report to Congress in which he stressed that 'Honduras' geographical position gives it a key role in preventing regional conflicts and potential infiltrations'. Shortly afterwards, *Washington Post* columnist Jack Anderson observed that the Carter administration had 'apparently chosen Honduras to be our new Nicaragua — a dependable satellite bought and paid for by American military and economic largesse'. Honduras did indeed replace Somoza's Nicaragua as Washington's most reliable ally in the region. But in practice, the choice was not difficult — Honduras was the only option available. Although both Guatemala and El Salvador possessed more efficient and professional armies, and the Guatemalan army had almost 20 years of counterinsurgency experience, the governments of both countries were facing serious social and political unrest. Moreover, US relations with both armies had deteriorated rapidly under Carter, who had cut off military aid in 1977 as a result of human rights violations. In contrast, Honduras faced no domestic insurgent movement, possessed an army that already enjoyed historically close relations with the US, and shared common borders with all three Central American republics.

But for the Carter administration, it was not simply a matter of finding a replacement for Somoza. They also wanted the Honduran army to play a role in the Salvadorean civil war. One of the many lessons of Nicaragua (for both the right and the left) was that Somoza had been seriously weakened by the half-hearted neutrality of Honduras. Many of the Honduran generals had remained at best indifferent during the defeat of Somoza, while some had made significant sums of money from selling arms to the Sandinistas. Carter's initial policy was to use Honduras as a defensive army of containment to form a *cordon sanitaire* around El Salvador.

Two of the main Salvadorean guerrilla organisations, the Popular Liberation Forces (FPL) in the department of Chalatenango and the Revolutionary Army of the Poor (ERP) in Morazán, had set up camps in the demilitarised pocket areas *(bolsones)* along El Salvador's border with Honduras, which had been established as a result of the 'football war' of 1969. When the Salvadorean army stepped up repression of these two organisations in early 1980, thousands of peasants were forced to flee into Honduras. At the same time, Honduras assumed greater importance as the guerrillas began using the country as a staging post for arms supplies bought in Europe and landed on Honduras' Atlantic coast.

By early 1980, Vaky's successor at the State Department, William Bowdler, was again stressing Honduras' key geopolitical position in the 'bridge-building process in Central America', but added ominously that 'Honduras should not be exploited as a conduit for the infiltration of men and arms to feed conflicts in neighbouring El Salvador and Nicaragua'. New training and equipment and increased levels of military aid were necessary to strengthen the Honduran army and prepare it for a role in US counterinsurgency strategies. But Carter did not want the embarrassment of working with another military despot. It was made clear to the Honduran armed forces that the US would increase military and economic aid to Honduras on condition that clean elections for a Constituent Assembly (not for the presidency) be held as scheduled in April 1980.

The elections were not intended to bring about any fundamental changes. In the absence of strong parties to the left of centre, the elections would be fought between the Nationalists and the Liberals, whose major policy differences were hard to identify. But it was the appearance of democratic rule that was crucial for Carter's national and international credibility. As one foreign diplomat remarked to the *New York Times* in April 1980, 'the vital thing is that no one be able to question the legitimacy of the next government'.

For the Honduran military, pressure to hold elections came neither as a great surprise nor a threat. Even before the Sandinista victory, the junta that had overthrown General Melgar Castro on 7 August 1978 had pledged to hold elections in 1980, reportedly on the promise of increased US aid. The overthrow of Somoza made the 'elections-aid' deal more urgent for both sides. Significant sectors of the Honduran army had been sobered by the rapid collapse of Somoza's National Guard, and at the same time recognised that public opinion was building up against 17 years of corrupt and inept military rule. The Carter administration, for its part, carefully nurtured the acquiescence of junta chief General Policarpo Paz García in the planned return to civilian rule. As early as September 1979, William Bowdler had been dispatched to Tegucigalpa in the first of a series of meetings between Paz and US officials both inside and outside Honduras.

US pressure proved effective. Amidst rumours that the National Party was preparing either a massively fraudulent electoral census or threatening a coup (with the possible support of Paz), Paz declared in March 1980 that the elections for the Constituent Assembly would be clean and honest. On 20 April, 81 per cent of registered voters turned out to vote, and the Liberals won a surprising 35 seats to the Nationalists' 33, with PINU (the Innovation and Unity Party) taking three. The victory was widely interpreted as a repudiation of military rule, as the National Party was notorious for its close connections with the armed forces. Although the military junta formally handed over power to the newly elected Constituent Assembly, the Liberals lost out in negotiations over the procedure for elections of a civilian president. Whereas the Liberals wanted the Assembly to elect a president, the Nationalists and PINU favoured a separate round of national elections. Since the Liberals did not have an overall majority of seats, a political stalemate ensued. As a way out of the impasse, the parties agreed on Paz as an interim head of state to oversee the 18-month period before the presidential elections in early 1982, and the army remained in political control of the country.

The Interregnum

The US was quick to offer its support to Paz. In fiscal year 1980, total economic aid to Honduras had already doubled to US$51 million, of which US$41 million came from USAID — a full 18 per cent of the Latin American total for that year. More significant was military aid. In April 1980, the same month as the elections, the Carter administration reprogrammed US$3.5 million for Foreign Military Sales (FMS) and increased International Military Education and

Training (IMET) grants to US$450,000. As part of an overall effort to increase the mobility of the Honduran army, ten Huey UH-1H helicopters were leased free of charge to the Honduran air force. In addition, a number of Green Beret advisers were dispatched to conduct training in 'tactical small group' and border security operations.

The Honduran army had done little to monitor the Sandinista guerrilla activity during the Nicaraguan civil war, but they now cracked down on the FMLN's supply lines. Steps were taken to increase Honduran co-operation with the Salvadorean army's counterinsurgency operations. The US was keen to secure some resolution of the border dispute between the two countries, both to facilitate joint operations and to allow the Salvadorean army access to the demilitarised border zones. In October 1980 a provisional agreement was signed, which was widely regarded as beneficial to El Salvador at a time when international opinion favoured Honduras. To many Hondurans, it was a clear indication of the willingness of the transitional government to go along with US plans. Although the treaty did not resolve the border demarcation dispute, it did provide for joint patrolling of the border, and granted the Salvadorean army access to the *bolsones* in pursuit of the guerrillas.

In fact, even before the treaty had been signed, joint operations between the two armies had already begun. In one notorious incident on 14 May 1980, some 600 Salvadoreans were killed trying to cross the Sumpul river, which divides the two countries, in an operation involving both armies. According to witnesses, peasants who tried to cross the river were forced back by Honduran soldiers to the zone of the massacre, where they were killed by the Salvadorean army. A document giving details of the river Sumpul massacre was signed by the bishop and 38 priests and religious from the frontier diocese of Santa Rosa de Copán, and caused considerable embarrassment to the government and a public outcry throughout Honduras. Ten months later in March 1981, a similar massacre of a large number of Salvadorean peasants took place as they fled across the river Lempa.

In the domestic political sphere, the period between April 1980 and the presidential elections of November 1981 was marked by a prolonged bout of jockeying both between the civilian politicians and the military and within the military establishment. Just as the military recognised that a freely elected civilian government was inevitable, so the leaders of both the National and Liberal parties lobbied for support amongst the generals. New alliances were formed and old ones strengthened. In August 1980, a purge of COSUFA (the Armed Forces' Superior Council) removed the more liberal and progressive army officers. A number of younger officers emerged to challenge the old guard represented by figures like Paz García and Melgar Castro. A group of seven officers, known locally as the 'iron circle', made their bids for power as Paz's retirement date approached. All of them had been trained in the Honduran military academy. They were strongly anti-communist, pro-US and receptive to the US demands that they should return to the barracks and cede formal political power to a civilian president.

Of these seven, three were strong favourites to take over from Paz: Colonel Humberto Bodden, commander of the 1st Infantry Battalion near Tegucigalpa; Colonel Leónidas Torres Arias, head of G-2 (military intelligence); and Colonel Gustavo Alvarez Martínez, chief of the public security forces (FUSEP) and the National Department of Investigations (DNI). Of the three, Bodden was thought to be the US favourite as long as Carter remained president. Although he generally supported US policy in the region, he was not as rigidly anti-communist as his main rival, Alvarez, who was notorious for his hatred of the Sandinistas and the FMLN, and had the support of the more right-wing sectors of the Honduran oligarchy and business sectors (see box below). Torres Arias was known to be close to Policarpo Paz, who had been adopting a relatively neutral position towards Nicaragua and El Salvador.

The Life and Times of Gustavo Alvarez

Training: included officer training courses at the National Military Academy in Argentina (1958-1962), and at the Superior War College in Peru; advanced infantry and counterinsurgency training at Fort Benning, Georgia and the School of the Americas in Panama; and police operations training in Washington under the Office of Public Safety programme (which was closed by Congress in the 1970s after allegations concerning the brutality of its training courses).

Positions held: Alvarez began his career as head of the 4th Infantry Battalion in La Ceiba, department of Atlántida, where Standard Fruit has its headquarters. He is best known as the officer who ordered the army to intervene and dismantle the banana co-operative of Las Isletas in 1977 — documents later revealed that he was authorised to receive US$2,850 from Standard Fruit prior to the raid. He later became head of military zone II in San Pedro Sula — in March 1979, he ordered the police to storm the Bemis Handal textile factory in San Pedro Sula. He was appointed chief of FUSEP (Public Security Forces) in 1980, which also gave him control of the secret police (DNI). He relied heavily on Argentine advisers in building up an efficient domestic security network. He is said to be a close friend of General Videla (president of Argentina during the so-called 'dirty war' from 1976-79), US multinationals like Standard Fruit, and the San Pedro Sula business community.

Ideology: while in Argentina, Alvarez was heavily influenced by the doctrine of national security; he has frequently expressed open admiration for the methods used by the Argentine military during the 'dirty war'; his favourite reading is said to be *Geopolitica* by the Chilean president, General Augusto Pinochet; according to a report in *Newsweek,* 'he doesn't care if officers are thieves, as long as they are virulent anti-communists'; in August 1982, Torres Arias (ex-head of Military Intelligence) denounced the 'extreme psychosis' of his former boss, accused him of having a 'plan of physical extermination of everyone who did not share his radical ideas', and charged him with 'leading Honduras into an abyss of internal destruction, and preparing the people for the possibilities of war with Nicaragua'; his two most frequently-quoted maxims are (i) 'there are only two types of politicians — communists and others', and (ii) 'everything you do to destroy a Marxist regime is moral.'

Source: Washington Office on Latin America, and EPICA task force (Washington).

What ensured Alvarez's eventual rise to the head of COSUFA was Reagan's election in November 1981. Alvarez's views were most in tune with the right-wing ideologues who dominated the thinking of the new Reagan administration, while his sharpness, professionalism and efficiency commended him to the pragmatists who dominated its practice. Even before the 1980 elections, he had held meetings with the country doctor and Liberal leader, Roberto Suazo Córdova. Suazo had sought connections with pro-US officers and he and Alvarez had drawn close together, assisted by the enmity between Alvarez and the Nationalist leader, Ricardo Zuñiga. By 1981 they had developed an intimate working relationship. As one observer remarked, 'independent of US interests . . . Alvarez and Liberal Party leaders met each others' needs'. The Liberal leader sought office, while Alvarez had his own political project. 'The personal friendship we have', Suazo Córdova was to comment two years later, 'no one will destroy. We could not be parted when God has brought us together'.

Election Fever

In the run-up to the 1982 presidential elections, the high command of the army was concerned that the newly elected Constituent Assembly might investigate military corruption. Civilian leaders however, knew only too well that some sort of understanding would have to be reached with the military for the elections to go ahead.

The military had good reasons to fear any civilian investigation. The major factor behind the removal of the last two military presidents had been revelations about corruption — López Arellano in 1975 for his alleged involvement in the US$1.25 million bribe from United Fruit, and Melgar Castro in 1978 for his connections with drug trafficking. Paz García himself had become widely known as 'Inca-Paz' ('incapable') because of the periodic interruption of government by his heavy drinking bouts. His enormous demand for hard liquor was reported to have been satisfied by his running a whisky-smuggling racket. But corruption spread wider than the presidents. During the Nicaraguan civil war, Paz's interior minister had displayed a heightened sense of neutrality by selling arms to the Sandinistas and intelligence to Somoza.

In early October 1981, a meeting was held in Tegucigalpa between the military high command and the leaders of the National and Liberal parties. The deal was struck: there would be no investigation into military corruption (which, the army claimed mysteriously, 'would play into the hands of the enemies of the country'); the military would retain a veto over Cabinet appointments; and there would be no civilian interference in military affairs, including national security, and any matter relating to Honduran borders.

However, there was still some doubt as to whether the elections would take place. Rumours circulated that the extreme right were again encouraging the military to intervene and were receiving a sympathetic hearing from Paz. The centre parties, the Christian Democrats and PINU, were calling for a postponement because of irregularities in the electoral rolls. The US and its allies in the army and Liberal Party lobbied to preserve the elections. Paz was discredited when news was leaked about a land scandal involving Paz's finance minister, Valentín Mendoza, and it was hinted that the scandal might extend to the presidential palace.

The Liberal Party, led by Suazo Córdova, went on to win the November elections by 100,000 votes, taking a 44-34 majority in the Assembly over the Nationalists. PINU took three seats while the Christian Democrats took one. A massive 80 per cent of the electorate turned out to vote. The Liberals again benefited from their reputation for anti-militarism. The editor of the main Honduran liberal newspaper, *Tiempo,* commented that 'it was a vote against corruption, and against the presence of the military in power. It was in favour of a change in political style, and in favour of neutrality in the regional war'. In fact, precisely at the moment that the electorate had voted that the generals should relinquish their control over Honduran politics, the military were strengthening their political position through the Suazo Córdova-Alvarez alliance. This in turn enabled the US to increase its influence over economic, political and military decisions. Honduras was dragged further into the regional turmoil of Central America.

The Reagan Plan

Until the November 1981 elections, the Reagan administration continued the Carter plan for Honduras. But the ideologues shaping Reagan's policies towards Central America had a fundamentally different conception of the root of the problem. Carter has at first tried to pursue political solutions to the conflict in Central America. In September 1979 his assistant secretary of state, Viron Vaky, had stated categorically that 'Castroist Marxist-Leninists could exacerbate the tension and violence in Central America, but they were not the ones who caused it'. Although by the end of his administration Carter's priorities had shifted towards traditional cold-war responses, Reagan's vision of Central America was, from the beginning, that of a battleground between East and West. November 1981 marked a new emphasis in US policy goals for Honduras. Honduras would remain a buffer state against the FMLN in El Salvador, but it would also be used as a springboard for the destabilisation of Nicaragua through a US-financed counterrevolutionary force and a base for US military operations in the region.

In the same month as the elections and in tacit recognition of the geopolitical importance now assigned to Honduras, the Reagan administration upgraded its embassy from grade four to grade two. Ambassador Jack Binns was replaced by John Dimitri Negroponte, a

82

skilled and experienced diplomat who had served extensively in South-East Asia, where he had gained a reputation as an uncomprising anti-communist. In 1965 he was among those urging President Johnson to increase US involvement in Vietnam; later he played a part in the secret bombing of Cambodia. Although the US magazine *Newsweek* did not break the story until a year later, November 1981 was also the month in which the National Security Council approved covert military operations against Nicaragua, whose long-term aim was to weaken and eventually unseat the Sandinista government. Negroponte would be the man in overall charge of the 'no-so-secret' war, while Honduras would be the centre of operations. A third significant, and related, event was the December statement by Assistant Secretary of State for Inter-American Affairs, Thomas Enders, that Cuba had successfully brought together a National Directorate of revolutionary organisations in Honduras which advocated armed struggle. As the Washington Office on Latin America (WOLA) reported, 'local observers, because of the reality of an historically splintered and isolated revolutionary movement there, found this hard to swallow'. In fact, a meeting between the Honduran left had apparently taken place around the time of the elections, but the result was a splintering into further divisions and not unification. The elections, Negroponte's arrival and Enders' statement were all preparations for the militarisation of Honduras.

Two months after Negroponte's arrival in Tegucigalpa, Alvarez was named head of COSUFA and duly confirmed in his position by the Liberal majority in the Assembly. In April 1982, Suazo further cemented his relationship with Alvarez by suddenly making him a brigadier general, altering the military codebook to allow his promotion, and getting the Constituent Assembly to show unanimous approval of the measure. Alvarez himself was said to have engineered the move, and the US embassy gave its blessing. Alvarez quickly dealt with his main rivals, Torres Arías and Bodden. With the imperious, *'O mando o no mando'* ('either I'm in charge or I'm not'), Alvarez dispatched Arías into diplomatic exile as military attache to Argentina and Bodden to Taiwan.

Over the next two years the Alvarez-Negroponte-Suazo triumvirate ruled Honduras. Power was concentrated in the executive and Honduras became an instrument of US plans in the region. Although there are arguments over the precise pecking order, each member of the triumvirate complemented the other. Suazo's role was to turn the Assembly into a rubber stamp for executive policy. Negroponte's relationship with Alvarez was never as crude as that of puppeteer to puppet. In fact they shared the same basic goals: a deep anti-communism and desire to bring down the Sandinista government.

The CIA's Creation

Because of the Congressional restrictions on the number of US troops operating abroad, initial efforts to put pressure on the Sandinistas focused on plans to resurrect CONDECA (the Central American Defence Council). A number of high-level meetings took place during 1981 between the head of the Southern Command, General Paul Gorman, and military leaders from Guatemala, El Salvador and Honduras. But the plans foundered when Guatemala's generals, engaged in their own counterinsurgency war, refused to fall in with them. Following the FMLN's military offensive in January 1981, the Salvadorean army too found itself tied up in its long war. Another plan to involve an inter-American intervention force disintegrated following the Falklands/Malvinas war. As a result, from mid-1982 onwards there was a definite shift of emphasis towards increasing support for the *contras* in Honduras, and, to a lesser extent, for those based in Costa Rica.

Following Somoza's overthrow in July 1979, a majority of the defeated National guardsmen had fled across the border into Honduras. Tolerated by the Honduran government during 1979-80, many could be seen enjoying Tegucigalpa's squalid night life, while their superiors took it easy in Miami, occasionally linking up with Cuban-run vice rackets. A few had begun the fight against the Sandinistas. From late 1980 to early 1981, the Nicaraguan government reported as many as 96 incursions along its northern border with Honduras. However, during Carter's administration, the *Somocistas* were weak, fragmented and demoralised. Had it not been for the arrival of Reagan in the White House, they would almost certainly have merged into the Caribbean underworld, just as the defeated Cuban army of Fulgencio Batista had done 20 years before.

Efforts were immediately made to weld the disparate groups of ex-Guardsmen into a unified and efficient guerrilla force. The US$19 million the National Security Council approved in November 1981, to support efforts to cut off alleged arms supplies from Nicaragua to the FMLN in El Salvador, went straight to CIA agents in Honduras who were mounting harassment operations against the Sandinistas in December 1981. With the active collusion of the Honduran military command, the CIA worked with Argentine military advisers to transform the various National Guard factions into a united organisation, the Nicaragua Democratic Force (FDN). FDN camps were set up in Honduran border departments, while Honduran army units provided logistical backup for the guerrilla operations.

A *Newsweek* story of November 1982 drew international attention to US ambassador Negroponte's personal role in the direction and co-

US marine guarding supply ship during Big Pine II.

ordination of the *contra* efforts. Together, the Honduran army, the US and the Argentine trainers ensured the military and political survival of the Somocistas. As for the exact division of labour between then, Edgar Chamorro, a former leader of the FDN, was later to reveal:

'The FDN was started with the cooperation of the Argentine advisers; the Hondurans who provided the territory, logistical support, military facilities, and some training; and the Americans, who gave the money and overall supervision. We called it *la tripartita*. The Hondurans were also very close to the FDN in the overall direction of the military operations. After the coup against Alvarez in March 1984, cooperation continued . . . the same colonel who had been the liaison with the FDN is still there, Col. Calderini.'

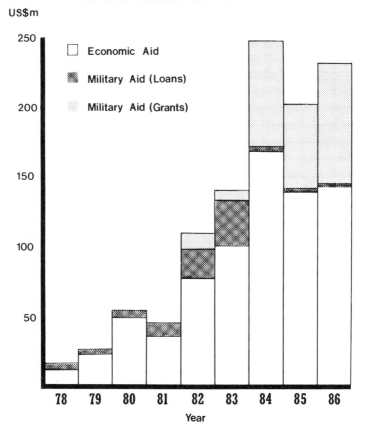

U.S. Aid to Honduras 1978 – 1986

US Economic and Military Assistance to Honduras 1978-1986 (US$ millions)

Year	ESF	DA/PL 480	Total econ.	MAP	FMS	IMET	Total milit.	Total aid
1978	—	13.0	13.0	—	2.5	0.7	3.2	16.2
1979	—	24.0	24.0	—	2.0	0.3	2.3	26.3
1980	—	50.7	50.7	—	3.5	0.45	4.0	54.7
1981	—	36.1	36.1	—	8.4	0.5	8.9	45.0
1982	36.8	41.3	78.1	11.0	19.0	1.3	31.3	109.4
1983	56.0	46.7	102.7	27.5	29.0	1.3	37.3	140.0
1984	112.5	56.2	168.7	77.5	—	1.0	78.5	247.2
1985	75.0	64.0	139.0	61.3	—	1.2	62.5	201.5
1986*	80.0	62.9	142.9	87.0	—	1.2	88.2	231.1

*proposed

Notes:
1. MAP = Military Assistance Programmes (grants); FMS = Foriegn Military Sales (loans); IMET = International Military Education and Training.
2. ESF (Economic Support Funds) is security supporting assistance for 'strategic economies', and is often treated as military aid; DA = Development Assistance distributed through AID; PL 480 = Food for Peace.

Source: US Congressional hearing on Honduras, February 1985.

The Pentagon Republic

The CIA support for the *contras* was initially a covert part of US operations in Honduras. More visible was the growing number of US troops in the country. In 1980 there were approximately 25 US military personnel in Honduras. Since the summer of 1983, the number of US troops did not drop below 700-800, and was often as high as several thousand. They were stationed in various military locations throughout Honduras, and were involved in a multitude of tasks ranging from training special anti-guerrilla units to operating radar stations. Their presence was the most obvious symbol of Honduras' status as the 'Pentagon Republic', but they constituted only one element in a massive programme of US-sponsored militarisation.

Large increases in US military and economic aid began in 1982. Agreements signed by Alvarez and Suazo in Washington in June of that year provided for major changes in the quantity and type of US aid (see box, p.87). In 1982, Honduras became the second largest recipient of US military aid in Latin America, receiving US$31.3 million for the financial year, when it had previously received only slightly more, US$32.5 million, for the whole of the period 1946-81. Between 1981 and 1986, there was a tenfold increase in military aid from US$8.9 million to US$88.2 million, while the money and equipment increasingly came in the form of gifts rather than loans. As for economic aid, Washington has provided Honduras with more than US$900 million since 1946, of which US$700 million was received between 1979 and 1986.

Initially, the joint US-Honduran military exercises resembled the manoeuvres which the US had traditionally practised in Central America. Short-term shows of strength were designed to develop co-ordination with friendly countries and improve the combat readiness of local armies. But soon the series of manoeuvres involved massive deployments of Honduran and US troops, lasting for much longer periods and with quite different purposes. Starting with Big Pine I in February 1983, there was a slow buildup in the number and frequency of joint operations. Some were short-term counterinsurgency operations which often involved a higher ratio of Honduran troops to US troops, but others were on a much grander scale. In May 1984, a series of major naval manoeuvres and land exercises brought 33,000 US troops to the region, while Big Pine III involved eleven weeks of continuous operations from February to May 1985 (for a full list of exercises, see appendix I). The purpose of these exercises was not just to intimidate the Sandinistas and prepare for a possible invasion. As a 1985 study by the US-based National Action and Research on the

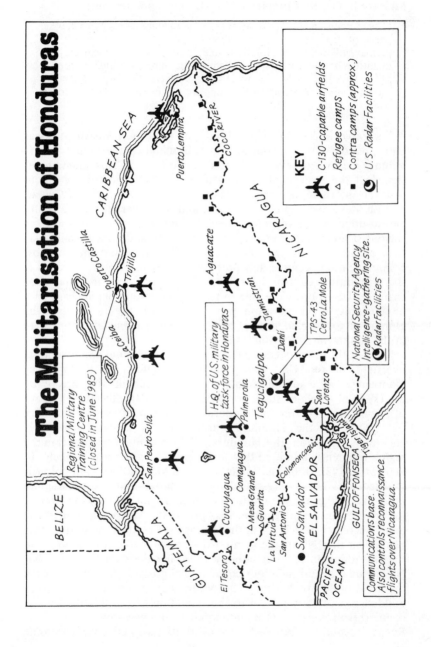

The Militarisation of Honduras

CARIBBEAN SEA

Puerto Lempira

COCO RIVER

NICARAGUA

Puerto Castilla

Trujillo

La Ceiba

Aguacate

Jamastrán

Danlí

TPS-43
Cerro La Mole

| National Security Agency. Intelligence-gathering site. ☾ Radar Facilities |

Regional/Military Training Centre (closed in June 1985)

San Pedro Sula

H.Q. of U.S. military task force in Honduras

Palmerola

Tegucigalpa

San Lorenzo

Comayagua

Cucuyagua

△ Mesa Grande
△ Guarita

Colomoncagua

El Tesoro
La Virtud
San Antonio

San Salvador

EL SALVADOR

GUATEMALA

BELIZE

Tiger Isl.

GULF OF FONSECA

Communications base. Also controls reconnaissance flights over Nicaragua.

PACIFIC OCEAN

Military Industrial Complex (NARMIC) has pointed out:

'The exercises in Honduras differ from US military manoeuvres in other parts of the world in that they involve construction which has permanently improved Honduran military facilities; they have left huge quantities of military equipment behind; they have paralleled the growth of the CIA-sponsored covert war against the Sandinistas; and some of the US built facilities and US equipment has been used for the covert war.'

The rapid improvement in Honduras' military infrastructure was only possible after an amendment was made to the bilateral 1954 military agreement between Honduras and the US. This amendment, signed at the request of Alvarez in May 1982, allowed the US to upgrade the three airports of Palmerola, Golosón (near La Ceiba), and La Mesa (near San Pedro Sula), and any other airport they later agreed upon. Three years later, ten air bases had been constructed in various strategic locations (see map, p.89). In addition, by mid-1984 two radar stations, a new military hospital and new roads, communications centres and port facilities had all been completed. But Honduran control over the US presence was minimal. For example, US troops were able to fly into the Palmerola air base with no customs or immigration procedures, with the result that the Honduran government did not even known how many US troops were in the country at any given time.

Most of the military construction took place without Congressional oversight in the US, while funds designated for the military manoeuvres were administered from special accounts run directly by the US joint chiefs of staff at the Pentagon. Officially, the objective of the military buildup in Honduras was to modernise the defensive capabilities of the Honduran armed forces against a possible Nicaraguan invasion. But Honduran and US military personnel in the region frequently admitted that was such an invasion was unlikely. In September 1982, John Buchanan, a retired Marine lieutenant-colonel, testified to a US congressional sub-committee that the Nicaraguan army had neither the ground forces, the tanks nor the back-up aircraft to make an invasion feasible. In April 1985, *Newsweek* quoted the under-secretary of defence at the Pentagon, Fred Ikle, as stating, 'the equipment that Nicaragua is importing is eminently suitable to crush the freedom fighters, but nobody following the data is saying that Nicaragua is acquiring major conventional ground offensive forces in the style of North Korea'. The Nicaraguan government's military buildup was directly related to the escalation of US support for the counterrevolutionary forces attempting to overthrow it. But the Reagan administration used it to justify its own military programme

US marines arriving for Big Pine II.

for the region. In the name of protecting Honduras' fragile democracy against the so-called aggression of its neighbour, the US was militarising the Honduran state and making the achievement of democracy more remote.

The Impact on Domestic Politics

The consolidation of the triumvirate of Suazo Córdova, Alvarez and Negroponte soon after the November 1981 elections defined domestic politics for the following three years. On the day of his nomination as the new head of COSUFA, Alvarez told the assembled press that he would supervise 'the rule of law and order to ensure the continued peace and tranquillity of the country'. His platitudes disguised the fact that Alvarez was arguably the first Honduran leader to have a coherent project for his country, based on the doctrine of national security, and the capacity to implement it. He managed to concentrate an extraordinary degree of power in his hands, and began by using it against the left-wing opposition movement. The support of the US embassy strengthened his position considerably and he was soon by-passing Congress and even the elected executive in a way which seriously undermined civilian politics and the democratic image fostered by the US and the Liberal government.

Popular organisations had felt the heavy hand of military repression before Alvarez arrived on the scene, but repression had never been part of a systematic policy as it was with Honduras' neighbours. Alvarez was influenced by the national security doctrine espoused by various military regimes throughout Latin America, which holds that the world is divided into just two blocs — Western Christendom and communism. According to this doctrine, the former is in a state of permanent war against the subversion by the latter; subversives are defined to include many of those who are simply opposed to the government; and the security forces are above scrutiny from any civilian government or judiciary. Even before the 1981 elections, Alvarez had begun to set up a sophisticated apparatus of repression necessary to enforce the doctrine. With Suazo as president, he now enjoyed the tacit acceptance of politicians and technocrats for the doctrine, which gave him more room to put it into practice. Civil defence committees, intelligence-gathering networks, and a new counterinsurgency unit known as the *cobras* were soon in full operation, all of them subject to his final authority.

As head of FUSEP and the DNI in 1980-81, Alvarez had already won himself a reputation for masterminding the disappearance of a number of Salvadoreans said to have links with the FMLN. Just prior to the November 1981 elections, there was a noticeable rise in human rights violations. This coincided with the period in which both local Honduran guerrillas and units of the FMLN carried out several kidnappings and murdered a San Pedro Sula businessman. The violations increased when the Suazo Córdova civilian government took office and when Alvarez was promoted to head of COSUFA. From that moment on, although never reaching the scale of the massacres occurring in Guatemala and El Salvador, a clear pattern emerged of selective disappearances, regular denial of *habeas corpus,* systematic torture and extrajudicial killings by government security forces and death squads (see chart below).

Human Rights Violations in Honduras 1980-1984

	1980	1981	1982	1983	1984*	Total
Political assassinations						
Hondurans	1	16	16	18	13	64
Salvadoreans	0	25	12	5	21	63
Other	0	1	1	2	2	6
Total	1	42	29	25	36	133
Permanently disappeared						
Hondurans	2	10	24	21	14	71
Salvadoreans	0	22	0	1	5	28
Other	0	20	2	3	0	25
Total	2	52	26	25	19	124
Temporarily disappeared						
Hondurans	11	64	33	18	30	156
Salvadoreans	0	3	2	0	0	5
Other	0	0	0	1	2	3
Total	11	67	35	19	32	164

Political prisoners
From 1980 to 1983 there were 58 political prisoners, of whom 44 were Hondurans, 9 Nicaraguans and 5 Salvadoreans. From January to November 1984, there were 160 political prisoners registered, of whom 16 were sent to court before 31 March 1984, and 144 after.

*Until November 1984.

Source: Committee for the Defence of Human Rights (CODEH).

For the first time in Honduran history, two human rights organisations were set up, CODEH (the Committee for the Defence of Human Rights) in 1981 and later, in 1982, COFADEH (the Committee of Families of the Detained-Disappeared). They and other human rights observers pointed out that throughout the period of the Suazo Córdova government the armed left in Honduras remained extremely marginal. Most of the victims of the abuses came from political or popular organisations working peacefully and openly for change. Alvarez's policy was widely regarded as a 'war of decapitation' against leaders of the more radical popular organisations.

The majority of human rights violations were carried out by the *cobras* and special 'hit squads' created by Alvarez and responsible to him alone. Officially, the Reagan administration claimed ignorance of the killings, but privately US advisers admitted to being well aware of what was happening. Mention of two left-wing Honduran politicians kidnapped in 1981 brought the response from the political officer at the US embassy in Tegucigalpa that they were 'pathological killers who deserved to be crushed like cockroaches'.

The Centre for Emergency Information

This proclamation appeared in the Honduran press on 23 September 1983

In the interests of national security, the Armed Forces of Honduras, through the Public Security Force (FUSEP) have created the Centre for Emergency Information (CIE) in order to help the Honduran people inform the various agencies concerned with state security about any attitude which they consider suspicious and that concerns security.

The Centre for Emergency Information will function on a national level and accept any information or denunciation of suspicious acts against the security of persons and institutions of the state.

To help the Honduran people inform the CIE, a system of telephone numbers has been developed, which we are making known to the public.

It is unnecessary for informers to give their name and identity when they call; it is up to them to identify themselves if they wish.

The telephone numbers which can be called are the following: *(There follows a list of towns and telephone numbers)*

The Centre for Emergency Information will work 24 hours a day and will give all due attention to emergency denunciations and calls made by responsible Hondurans who seek the peace and tranquillity of Honduras.

Bureau of Public Relations, Armed Forces of Honduras.

Alvarez also took steps to improve the state's information on the activities of political opponents. In July 1982 the government created civil defence committees, which were in effect networks of *orejas* (literally, 'ears'), whose function was to spy on their neighbours and report 'unusual activities' to the police or army. 'Centres for Emergency Information' (CIEs) were set up where people could bring their information and military personnel manned special telephone lines round the clock to receive denunciations. The centres were widely advertised in the pro-government press (see box opposite). The Honduran bishops declared in a statement in October 1982 that 'they did not know of such Committees being organised in any country that boasted of being democratic'.

A mission to Honduras organised by the US human rights group, Americas Watch, in December 1982 reported that 'the practice of arresting individuals for political reasons, and then refusing to acknowledge their whereabouts and status, seems to have become established in Honduras'. The report added that many of the disappeared had been taken to clandestine prisons where they had been subjected to various forms of torture. Writs of *habeas corpus* issued on behalf of the disappeared met a wall of silence from the authorities. But when six of the 'disappeared' turned up alive in late May and June, accounts of their torture and detention in secret prisons were widely publicised (see box, p.96). Although General Alvarez was ultimately responsible for the human rights abuses, a number of civilian politicians were well aware of what was going on. When, after Alvarez's fall in March 1984, the ex-minister to the presidency, Carlos Flores Facussé, accused Alvarez of all the abuses, Alvarez was quick to reply that his actions were carried out with the consent, knowledge and orders of President Suazo Córdova.

Congress Ignored

A series of legal changes were introduced to facilitate the crackdown on the opposition. Decree no.33 of April 1982, known as the anti-terrorist law, laid down jail sentences of 20 years and upwards for 'subversion', which included such traditional forms of protest as land takeovers, factory occupations and street demonstrations. At the same time, pro-government 'democratic fronts' were financed within trade unions where left-wing influence was strong, provoking divisions which could then be resolved in the government's favour by the law. During 1981, these 'democratic fronts' won control of both the United Fruit workers' union, SITRATERCO, and the university students' union. In November 1982, legal recognition was withdrawn

Testimony of Torture

Inés Consuelo Murillo, a 24-year-old law graduate, was captured by security forces on 13 March 1983 and held without trial for 80 days. Interrogation sessions were conducted by specialised personnel, whom she took to be army intelligence officers. On 30 May she was transferred to the DNI HQ, before her arrest was publicly acknowledged. She spent the next thirteen months in a public jail, before pressure from West German parliamentarians (Inés holds dual Honduran-German citizenship) secured her release. After paying a fine of nearly £1,500, she left Honduras for West Germany.

Capture at gunpoint

I was captured on Sunday 13 March 1983 at 6pm, as I was returning home after a game of chess with a doctor friend in Choloma. I was on my way to catch the bus to San Pedro Sula when suddenly a car tried to run us down (I was with an old man). The men inside the car, who were dressed as civilians, shouted, 'Stop! we are immigration officials'. The only credentials they had were their guns, which they pointed at us. I started to ask what was happening, but as I did so they grabbed my handbag and hit me in the face with the butt of their guns. They pushed us both into the car — by now the old man was paralysed with fright. I felt desperate as they started to beat us up inside the car. Then they blindfolded us and pushed us down on the floor of the car so as not to arouse suspicion among passers-by.

Secret jails

We were taken to the basement of a private house in San Pedro Sula and stripped of our clothes and possessions. They tied us up in the 'iguana' position, with hands and feet wrenched backwards and tied together behind us, and thrown into a pit. This was a form of treatment that was to be repeated frequently. Often we were hung up all night in the 'iguana' position .

I soon realised that we were being held by the military. I could hear the sound of army radio communications. Later I was to be shown a photograph of myself taken some four months before and distributed to the security police as a 'suspicious foreigner' visiting San Pedro Sula. Eventually I realised that I was being accused of involvement in a plot to kill the Pope during his Central American tour in early 1983.

From the first day of my arrest I was sexually abused and subject to psychological as well as physical torture. There were times when I thought I could stand no more, but whenever I considered signing a confession to put an end to my suffering, I thought of my family, and the implications for them. When they hung me from the ceiling they took care to wrap my wrists with strips of rubber, taken from inner tubes, so as to leave no marks. The old man was not so lucky, and the skin was torn from his wrists. When they torture you, you cry out, despite their attempts to cover your mouth. It is difficult to maintain conditions of secrecy in these places, because the cries of the victims are audible. As a result, I became aware of the presence of many others, although since I was blindfolded I never saw them. I tried desperately not to hear their screams — listening to the torture of others is the worst form of psychological torture.

During my 80-day disappearance I was held in two different private houses, both of which had secret prisons in their basements. Families lived on the upper floors, and one day I heard a woman call her husband and children for tea.

Release

Some ten days before I was shown to the press, I began to receive food in reasonable and regular quantities for the first time, and I was also given medicines. My wounds, however, were not attended to until I was transferred to a women's prison. Minutes before the press conference I was given some old clothes to put on — the only remnants of my own clothing were my shoes. I had been kept totally naked for 80 days. Naturally, it was not until my transfer to prison that I became aware of the international pressure for my release. Thanks to my mother's German nationality, I was one of the lucky ones.

Source: Central America Report no.19, London, 1984.

from the majority tendency of the main primary school teachers' union, COLPROSUMAH, and awarded to a minority, pro-government fraction.

Congress no longer had a role as a balancing force against abuse of executive authority. Suazo's *rodista* henchmen regularly delivered a majority in the Assembly on key pieces of legislation. Congress frequently refused to set up committees to investigate the regular denunciations of human rights violations, while the anti-terrorist law (which violated the Constitution) and the bill which made Alvarez head of the armed forces (which required an amendment to the Constitution) were all passed without adequate prior notice or time for debate. Only Efraín Díaz, the sole Christian Democrat deputy, was prepared to speak out in protest. In mid-1983 he told interviewers in Washington:

'The great problems that afflict Honduran society, namely problems of human rights, foreign policy and the economy are rarely debated in the Congress. The Congress legitimises all the executive wants. In other words, it is not, practically speaking, an independent power; it does not maintain any control over the executive.'

Díaz's point was most clearly demonstrated in the case of the establishment of the new regional training centre (the CREM) at Puerto Castilla on Honduras' Atlantic coast (see map, p.89). Since 1981 the US government had embarked on an ambitious training programme of middle-ranking Salvadorean officers, but they needed a cheaper location for a training centre than the US itself. The installation of the CREM was never debated in Congress, despite the fact that it involved an amendment of the Honduran-US military treaty of 1954. An agreement was made secretly between Alvarez and Negroponte in May 1983 to avoid popular protest arising from traditional anti-Salvadorean sentiment.

It was only after the first contingent of US trainers had actually arrived at the base in June 1983 that the issue was discussed by Honduran deputies. When it was pointed out that training foreign troops on Honduran soil would violate the Constitution, the wording of the bill was changed: Salvadorean soldiers were referred to as 'students', and the US military instructors as 'advisers'. Congress duly passed the legislation by 78 votes to 3, though the training of Salvadorean soldiers would remain a controversial issue for many members of the Honduran military. Meanwhile, the presence of US Green Berets in Puerto Castilla brought back particular memories for some US journalists. 'If it were not for the Spanish that floats from the tents', wrote the *Washington Post* correspondent in September 1983, 'this could be Vietnam.'

Reaganomics for Honduras

As in the military and political sphere, the policy prescriptions for the Honduran economy came virtually direct from the US embassy. A package of 'free market' measures based on 'Reaganomics' was

Tiempo

Suazo Cordóva.

John Dimitri Negroponte.

Tiempo

Walter López Reyes.

introduced following the November elections. The key element was the attraction of private investment, mostly from foreign sources. There was little discussion or action on social reform. As Teófilo Trejos, vice-president of UNACOOPH (the National Union of Popular Cooperatives) complained:

> 'The absence of resources for agrarian reform is ridiculous. There is plenty of money to build military airports, construct ports and buy arms. Here you have the spectacle of military manoeuvres which cost millions in the very zones, like the south, where peasants are dying of hunger.'

In the late 1970s, increased government spending, made possible by cheap borrowing on the Euromarket, and high commodity prices for Honduran exports had provided some temporary relief to the generally poor performance of the Honduran economy. GNP grew by 7.0 per cent in 1978 and 6.6 per cent in 1979. But efforts to diversify the economy and create a national industrial sector failed completely. As outlined in chapter 4, the institution set up to encourage this process, CONADI, had fallen prey to the corrupt practices endemic in Honduran economic life. When the business climate deteriorated sharply after the Nicaraguan revolution, CONADI's creditors simply ran off with the money to Miami, thus contributing to a capital flight of some US$600 million between 1979 and 1982. By 1982, CONADI had written off a large percentage of its US$175 million in debts, while the tab was picked up by the government, contributing to an ever increasing debt service burden.

The commodity price boom of the mid-1970s had just as suddenly turned into a price slump by the end of the decade. High import costs, an overvalued currency and critical shortage of foreign exchange further crippled the economy, while increasing US interest rates exacerbated the burden of the public sector debt. GNP growth dropped to 2.2 per cent in 1980, 0.3 per cent in 1981 and was negative (-1.4 per cent) in 1982.

Suazo's first Cabinet was dominated by representatives of precisely those business groups responsible for the capital flight. The Facussé family, whose chemical and agribusiness companies had borrowed heavily from CONADI and were now deeply in debt, figured prominently. Miguel Facussé was Suazo's economic adviser, and Carlos Facussé his leading political adviser. A widely publicised memorandum prepared by Miguel Facussé argued that the only way out of the national crisis was to 'sell Honduras to the foreign investor'. The other main intellectual source for the plan of economic revitalisation came from the US embassy. Even before the November elections, the Liberal Party had sought its advice, and four days after

Suazo's inauguration, Ambassador Negroponte handed him a remarkably direct memorandum containing a package of recommendations. The main components of the two memoranda were included in the economy minister's March 'Plan of Action'. The aim was to stimulate private investment, boost exports and deregulate the economy. It included measures to reduce public spending by 10 per cent, with drastic cuts in the budgets of the ministries of health, education, agrarian reform, transport and public works; to put an end to price controls for staples like milk, bread, medicine and eggs; to encourage more foreign tax exemption schemes; and to increase consumer and income taxes.

The steps were also perfectly in line with the policy recommendations of the IMF and the World Bank, who were willing to give generous amounts of aid to rescue the Honduran economy. Honduras received US$424.4 million in aid from the World Bank, the IMF and the Inter-American Development Bank in 1982 alone. The injection of foreign aid was supposed to keep Honduras solvent and also to shift the economy away from import substitution industries towards 'export-led' industrialisation aimed at US markets. The influx of money did not, however, improve the country's economic performance. Much of it was siphoned off before it could be used for purposes of national development. In early 1985, *Tiempo* reported that the Reagan administration feared that 'between 80 and 90 per cent of aid finds its way back to private accounts in North America'.

From mid-1981, Facussé and other leading businessmen set about trying to forge a multi-class coalition to put political weight behind the economic strategy. In January 1983, APROH (the Association for the Progress of Honduras) received its legal title from Suazo Córdova. APROH was a classic corporativist body linking together businessmen, the armed forces (represented by General Alvarez himself, as president), the rector of the national university and some conservative trade union leaders from the AFL-CIO-affiliated labour union, the CTH, and the peasant union, ANACH. For the next twelve months, APROH became the key axis of military/private-sector influence over economic and foreign policy issues, and brought a greater unity to the Honduran right than had ever been achieved by the traditional parties.

The economic model involved wage restrictions to attract foreign investment to the country. Control of trade union militancy was thus central to the economic project, and dovetailed with Alvarez's efforts to decapitate the more radical sectors of the union movement. In fact, APROH was seen as complementary to Alvarez's doctrine of national security. 'APROH's objective is to fight Marxism with ideas', explained APROH's executive secretary, Benjamín Villanueva, in

101

August 1983, 'Alvarez does it in other ways'. In early 1984, APROH's influence was so extensive that the Christian Democrat deputy, Efraín Díaz, could pronounce that it was 'the centre of power in Honduras'. It did not however, survive the downfall of its main guarantor, General Alvarez.

6 The Pact Reconsidered

At the end of March 1984, General Alvarez's political mission was brought to an abrupt end. Accused of corruption, warmongering and dictatorial behaviour, the armed forced chief was bundled onto a plane by his fellow officers and dispatched into exile. They had ousted from power Reagan's staunchest ally in Central America. However, Alvarez's captors were no radicals, and under their leadership Honduras continued to follow in its essentials the economic, political and military model elaborated by Alvarez, Suazo and Negroponte. The officers now in power claimed a certain amount of independence from the US, but they did not question Honduran subordination to the goals of US military strategy in the region. Their objective was to negotiate better terms in return for the maintenance of Honduras' role in the Reagan administration's regional strategy. As one military observer put it, 'If we have to suffer the political consequences of being a US base, we want a better price.'

The bargaining centred on five related issues: the future of the CREM training centre; the continued presence of the *contras*; the original terms of the 1954 military pact; the privileged treatment of the Salvadorean army; and a settlement of the border dispute with El Salvador. By mid-1985, the CREM training centre had been closed down, some restrictions had been put on *contra* activity, and a series of alterations to the 1954 treaty had been discussed. But the joint military manoeuvres, the buildup of the Honduran army and the expansion of the military infrastructure continued apace. The 'nationalism' of the new military commanders was widely regarded as a desire to wave the flag rather than rock the boat.

After Alvarez's departure, the return to the more cumbersome style of collegiate military leadership did not mean any reduction in military dominance over civilian politics. The *suazocordovista* faction of the Liberal Party was content to enter into a close, though still

103

subordinate, relationship with the new military high command. A major constitutional crisis in March 1985, prompted by internal Liberal Party feuding, exposed the fragility of Honduran 'democracy', and was only resolved in May under pressure from the army, the US and the trade unions. As in the past, the Honduran elites proved incapable of developing a stable system of parliamentary democracy.

Despite the decline of APROH after Alvarez's removal, the government remained committed to economic liberalisation. By mid-1985, it was clear that the economic model was a disastrous failure. But in the absence of any domestic political force capable of offering a serious challenge to the current political and socioeconomic model, the key to Honduras' destiny, as so often in the past, still lay beyond its borders.

The Fall of Alvarez

Just before midday on 31 March 1984, a West Wing plane carrying General Alvarez landed in San José, the capital of Costa Rica. Theories abound as to the exact reasons for his downfall. Corruption, human rights abuses, the flouting of Honduran sovereignty, and links with bizarre religious sects all created discontent within the officer corps. But one issue eventually united them against him: his thinly disguised drive for absolute power.

General Alvarez had remained true to the tradition of corruption among Honduran leaders. Although presented as a model of incorruptibility by his US backers, Alvarez used his executive powers to amass a considerable personal fortune, even directing funds from US economic and military aid into his own bank account. He enjoyed a wide range of business interests, including a principal shareholding in the US-based Union Star company, which exported arms, liquor and other products to the Honduran army. The officers who eventually threw him out had written evidence that he and other generals close to him (such as Bali Castillo and Bueso Rosa) had embezzled US$30 million of public funds. One of his clique, the head of the navy, General Rubén Humberto Montoya, was described by Negroponte as 'the open book of corruption in Honduras'. A boat built with US aid was reported to have cracked during trials to test its resistance to fire because Montoya had reduced the boat's specifications in order to pocket US$300,000.

Alvarez's ideological fanaticism also created concern amongst his opponents. In the belief that the biggest danger to Honduran security came from the Sandinistas and the FMLN, Alvarez was prepared to bring the country to the brink of war with Nicaragua. In December 1983 he boasted that he would spend his next birthday in Managua, sending shivers down the spines of junior officers who would actually be in charge of taking on the Sandinista army. Despite many officers' anti-Salvadorean sentiments, Alvarez had also stepped up collaboration with the Salvadorean army, and personally negotiated behind the backs of both the army and the elected government the agreement which established the CREM training centre. In addition, his messianic vision of his historical role as the liberator of the Western world at times made him an uncomfortable ally for the US when the situation demanded more subtle diplomacy. For example, in August 1982 Alvarez was encouraged by his Argentinian advisors to put the Honduran army on maximum alert, and was only dissuaded from invading Nicaragua by US pressure.

Many officers were also worried about the repercussions of the 'dirty war' against left-wing organisations in Honduras. In early 1984 there was a resurgence of labour repression when the Honduran army took over the running of the country's power stations in late March and arrested nearly 300 workers from the Union of the National Electric Energy Company (STENEE), who were protesting against the disappearance of their leader, Rolando Vindel. Some officers feared that a future civilian government might be less servile than Suazo's and seek to bring errant soldiers to justice.

Finally, Alvarez's flirtation with the Unification Church (commonly known as the Moonies) brought considerable consternation both to the loyally Catholic business elites in APROH and to some high-ranking officers. Alvarez promoted the sect and its political arm, the Confederation of Associations for the Unity of American Society (CAUSA), because it vigorously espoused his own simplistic and semi-mystical East-West view of the world. During 1983 the Honduran press publicised at length Alvarez's connections with two Moonie leaders, the South Koreans Sun Myung Moon and Bo Hi Pak. The liaison was particularly ill-considered since it clashed with Suazo's own attempts to champion Catholic sentiment and undermined APROH's claims to be the principal barrier against the atheistic tendencies of the left. Moreover, it caused some embarrassment to Negroponte. In 1983 the leader of the sect, Rev. Moon, was arrested in the US on tax evasion charges and was subsequently imprisoned.

Nevertheless, these issues alone would have been insufficient to halt the Alvarez bandwagon. Eventually, enough military officers were mobilised against him through distrust of his political ambitions. The last straw was his attempts in early 1984 to reorganise and centralise the army's command structure in his favour. Since its professionalisation in the 1950s, power in the armed forces had rested with COSUFA, which Alvarez believed to be both unwieldy and a potential limit on his own power. In March 1984, he presented a bill to Congress which would have reduced the size of COSUFA from 45 to 21 officers and established a new all-powerful council of eight senior military commanders. At the same time, he planned to lengthen the service period between the ranks of colonel and general and raise the minimum age for promotion to general to 55. These changes would have excluded from power the colonels, lieutenant-colonels and majors of the 6th and 7th promotions of the War College, and virtually all the infantry battalion commanders who had direct authority over troops. These measures were particularly galling to the officers who remembered that Alvarez had himself flouted the military codebook to become a general in April 1982.

After a stormy meeting of COSUFA in mid-March, an agreement to get rid of Alvarez was reached between most of the middle-level officers and some of Alvarez's former high-ranking allies, such as General Walter López and Colonel Roberto Martínez (see box opposite). On 31 March, Saturday-night radio and TV were interrupted by martial music and the news that Alvarez had resigned. Four other generals and a colonel were also removed. Neither Negroponte nor Suazo Córdova had been behind the coup. In fact, there were strong rumours that the plotters wanted to remove Suazo as well as Alvarez because of the civilian government's inept handling of the country's social and economic crisis. When Suazo questioned the constitutionality of Alvarez's removal, he was informed that the alternative was for him to join Alvarez on the plane to Costa Rica.

All Change, No Change

The United States accepted rather than welcomed the coup. It was soon clear that the new military hierarchy would change the emphasis rather than the content of Honduran foreign policy. On 26 May 1984, scarcely two months after Alvarez's removal, the new head of the armed forces, General Walter López Reyes, announced in an interview with the *Washington Post* that Honduras wanted to modify the 1954 military treaty with the US. It was the first sign that the Honduran army demanded a better deal from the Reagan administration, and the opening gambit in a long process of renegotiation. The desire to reconsider the pact stemmed from a cross-current of tendencies within the armed forces. Some feared that the US would abandon Honduras *à la* Vietnam, others that Honduras

106

How They Removed Alvarez

A small nucleus of lieutenant-colonels and majors, all of the sixth and seventh promotions of the War College, had been weaving a secret plot to oust Alvarez for three months. The conspiracy, at first planned for Holy Week, was hatched with such care that it passed unnoticed by the hundreds of CIA eyes and ears. During the week starting 18 March, there was a stormy meeting of COSUFA. One of its members questioned Alvarez about the disappearance of US$1 million earmarked for the purchase of military equipment. Alvarez was furious. At first he agreed to an investigative committee, but then he lashed into his subordinates, threatening them with the sack.

Alvarez only succeeded in creating a consensus against him. He severed his alliance with the old-guard colonels, which led officers like General Walter López and Colonel Roberto Martínez to join the conspiracy. General López demanded that the US be informed of the coup and met ambassador Negroponte one week before the crisis unfolded. Washington received the information and let things run — Alvarez's messianic warmongering was already proving inconvenient for Reagan in his reelection campaign.

On Friday 30 March, Alvarez decided to go to San Pedro Sula. In the evening, he chaired an assembly of APROH in the Chamber of Commerce in which 127,000 lempiras (US$63,500) were raised, mostly in cheques. According to reliable sources, Alvarez insisted that evening on the impossibility of coexisting with the Sandinistas and the proximity of war.

Saturday, D-Day

At 7 a.m. on the Saturday, D-Day, he arrived at the Armando Escalón air base where his special plane was waiting for him. He did not know that the main barracks at Tegucigalpa had been occupied that morning by 100 *cobras* under Lieutenant Colonel Mario Amaya. Three thousand other soldiers surrounded the capital.

Alvarez was met at the air base by Colonel Roberto Martínez and the chief of the base, Major Israel Navarro. Martínez greeted him with the words: 'My general, there's a call from the president.' It was a trick to separate him from his bodyguard. Major Navarro, a member of the inner circle of conspirators, accompanied him to the office. Once there, he told him that he was under arrest, and asked him to hand over his weapon and draw up his resignation. The general reacted angrily and asked the reason for his dismissal. He was told that it was because of corruption, the disappeared and the paramilitary groups. ▶

Tears of a Friend

Alvarez himself ordered his bodyguard not to resist. The only baggage he carried was a small case with the 127,000 lempiras he had collected the night before in the APROH meeting. The majority of signatories went to the banks first thing Monday morning to cancel the cheques.

The flight from San Pedro Sula to Tegucigalpa takes scarcely 20 minutes. The pilot of Alvarez's plane was his friend, Colonel Carlos Aguirre, who was admitted into the circle of conspirators at the last moment. They say that he cried when he saw his boss in handcuffs. The plane landed around 8 a.m. at the Hernan Acosta Mejía airbase, the main air force barracks. From there, the top generals were summoned by the high command. The first to get the call was the head of the joint chiefs of staff, General Abdenego.

The chief of the security forces, General Daniel Bali Castillo replied that he did not think he could make the appointment. On the other end of the phone they told him that if he did not turn up, they would bombard the police barracks, and if they caught him alive, he would be shot. The last one to be summoned was the chief of the navy, Rubén Humberto Montoya. When faced with his written resignation, he tried to protest: 'Why me?' The answer was explosive: 'Because you're a thief.'

Suazo, too?

With the four signed resignations in his pocket, General Walter López now phoned President Suazo, and invited him to come to the air force barracks for an urgent meeting with COSUFA. On arrival, the president was surprised to see only López and Colonels Erik Sánchez and Said Speer (who, as commanders of tank units, were key figures in the coup). López explained the situation to Suazo and handed him the document with Alvarez's resignation. The president argued that this was unconstitutional, but they replied that it was Alvarez who was acting against the constitution.

When the president resisted, one of the colonels left the meeting to consult with his colleagues waiting in another office. The decision was not long in coming. 'If you do not accept this arrangement, the plane is still waiting. You can accompany Alvarez to Costa Rica.'

Alvarez was taken to the president's West Wing plane and flown to San José between 10 and 11 a.m. Just before midday, he arrived in the Costa Rican capital, looking tired and unshaven. Later he would complain that they had treated him like a criminal. Back in Tegucigalpa, his family was expecting him for a christening. His wife was told that he had been kidnapped by a left-wing commando group. A few minutes later, all the radio stations in Honduras transmitted a military communiqué, announcing Alvarez's resignation.

Source: Adapted from *El País,* 6 April 1984.

would be drawn into a war with Nicaragua, and others again that Honduras had not secured a good enough deal from the US. But despite the new assertion of 'national dignity', the military leaders who replaced Alvarez did not disagree with the overall direction of foreign and domestic policy established by Suazo's government. The new general was firmly, rather than rabidly, anti-communist, and was willing to remain a close ally of the US.

The first issue concerning many of the officers was the future of the CREM training centre at Puerto Castilla. The first request was that the proportion of two Salvadoreans to every one Honduran trained at the base should be altered to an equal, or greater number of Hondurans. Despite 15 years of peace between the two countries since the 1969 'soccer war', many Hondurans still viewed the Salvadorean army as a greater threat to their sovereignty than the Sandinistas. As one officer candidly explained to the *Sunday Times* in February 1985, 'the Salvadoreans have still not killed enough of each other in their civil war . . . they still want more living room, and Honduras is their obvious target'.

El Salvador's privileged relationship with the US was especially resented by the military and politicians alike. As the new minister to the presidency, Ubodoro Arriga, pointed out, 'Honduras pays a valuable service to North American interests, but receives only half the economic aid and a third of the military aid of El Salvador'. The stakes were raised on 28 September when Honduras blocked the admission of Salvadorean troops to the CREM, pending a resolution to the impasse over the border dispute. The CREM was finally closed down completely in June 1985.

The second major issue was the presence of the *contras*. When in mid-1984 the Reagan administration's request for a further US$28 million for funding the *contras* was rejected three times by Congress, the Honduras army grew increasingly concerned about the future of the 10,000-15,000 *contras* on their soil. They insisted that, should Congressional funding not be reinstated, the US should assume responsibility for removing or otherwise dealing with the mercenaries. The *contras'* failure to capture and hold one single Nicaraguan village exacerbated their worries. As one senior Honduran officer put it, 'If they are guerrillas, why aren't they in the mountains? They are a bunch of dilettantes, who spend their lives in their casino. They will never overthrow the Sandinistas.' In early August 1984, the FDN hospital at Tamara was ordered to be closed, along with their command centre at Lepaterique. Later on 9 January 1985, Steadman Fagoth, the head of the MISURA group of Indian *contras,* was expelled after holding a press conference in Tegucigalpa — previously, this would have merited only a gentle warning. But the various moves to restrict the *contras* were mainly a reminder to the US that, like the CREM, their presence was another bargaining chip for the Hondurans. In fact, the *contras* were regularly told by Honduran officers merely to keep a lower profile, while all the time regular supplies and support were being flown in by the CIA from bases at Jamastrán and Aguacate.

The main objective for the Honduran officers was a massive increase in military and economic aid and a reworking of the 1954 treaty. The first demand was for US$1,700 million (US$1,300 million in economic aid, US$400 million in military aid) before the end of the 1980s, and twelve F-5E sophisticated combat jets. The last request was rejected outright, while in December 1984 the Reagan administration finally announced that it was asking Congress for a mere US$2.2 milion extra on its original request of US$86 million of military aid for FY 1986. The Honduran government's diplomatic efforts were revealed to be a dismal failure. As *Tiempo* commented, 'in the face of classic North American opportunism, the government has sold its birthright for a mess of pottage'. A personal visit to Washington by Suazo and López in May 1985 did not produce any additional aid, despite raising their original request to a massive US$3,000 million over the next four years. Nor did they get far with trying to change the terms of the 1954 treaty which gave the US complete freedom to conduct the military manoeuvres. The Hondurans wished to turn the treaty into a bilateral defence pact, but the US merely restated its multilateral obligations under the 1947 Rio Treaty. Minor changes were made to the 1982 annex (including Honduran jurisdiction over US troops), but these represented a tacit acceptance of a permanent US military presence in Honduras.

Suazo returned from Washington to announce that 'Honduran dignity had been rescued'. But in reality, over twelve months of intensive renegotiation had achieved very little. The fundamental reason for this 'undeclared defeat' was their unwillingness to play their most powerful bargaining card: Honduras' strategic position in the region. Instead, they were only prepared to tamper with the terms of their surrender to the US in an attempt to extract more money. As one US diplomat said of the Honduran demands, 'most of this is smoke. The new bunch is trying to show they are in charge to get at Alvarez. But we haven't been turned down on anything we've asked from them.'

The result was that the militarisation of Honduras continued unabated. The joint manoeuvres of Big Pine III in March-April 1985 involved 11,000 US and Honduran troops, and by mid-1985 there were at least 11,000 US personnel permanently stationed in the country. The Central American weekly *Inforpress* reported in

US adviser training Salvadorean soldier at the CREM, Puerto Castilla.

September 1985 that a new military base named Bulldog was under construction in the department of Yoro, which took the number of military bases in the country to thirteen. There was no sign that the US was intending to pull out in the near future. The *Washington Post* of 17 July 1985 quoted an internal Pentagon document as stating that the US manoeuvres would last at least another five years, until 1990. To quote Jorge Arturo Reina, a leader of MOLIDER, the US still had 'its eyes on Nicaragua, its hands in El Salvador and its feet in Honduras'.

On the domestic front, the new military leaders preserved the counterinsurgency structures and the framework of 'constitutional rule'. Although Alvarez's death squads were reined in, the civil defence committees and the specialised counterinsurgency forces were kept in operation. The new military leadership made an obvious effort to improve its human rights image by publicly denouncing abuses, meeting with human rights groups and setting up a committee to investigate past violations. As a gesture of intent, in August 1984 Captains Alexander Hernández and Alonso Canales, both of them linked to death-squad operations, were sent into exile, and several policemen said to be responsible for torture were dismissed.

But the human rights groups remained sceptical about the seriousness of the army's concern over abuses. When an armed forces' communiqué of 29 December 1984 announced the results of its investigations, that scepticism was justified. The report claimed to account for the whereabouts of only eight missing persons. The other 100 who had disappeared, the report stated, 'were possibly the victims of a vendetta carried out by non-Honduran armed leftist and rightist groups'. The 1984 survey by CODEH revealed that disappearances, illegal detentions and assassinations had continued after Alvarez's removal. Only the rate of political assassinations actually declined after March (see box below). 1985 saw no improvement — from January to July, according to CODEH, 21 more people disappeared.

Human Rights Violations in 1984		
	Jan.-March*	April-Nov.**
Political assassinations	21	15
Disappearances	5	14
Temporary disappearances	2	30
Political prisoners	16	144
Tortured	7	24

*Armed forces under General Alvarez
**Armed forces under General López

Source: Committee for the Defence of Human Rights (CODEH).

Democracy, Honduran-style

The smooth functioning of the Honduran parliamentary system raised considerable difficulties for the new leaders. The constitutional crisis of March 1985 threatened to destroy the democratic image which they were anxious to maintain. The army and the US, as the real wielders of power in the country, were forced to exert enough pressure on the party bosses to maintain stability.

Alvarez's personality and dictatorial style had masked the fact that Suazo and his Liberal Party faction ruled the party in a centralised and sectarian manner. Until the fall of Alvarez, the main alliance within the Liberal Party had been between the right-wing, urban-based technocrats (who supported politicians like José Azcona del Hoyo and Carlos Montoya) and the rural small landowners and traders (who backed the president). With the relaxation in political tension that followed the coup, the alliance began to fall apart.

The causes of the division were threefold: first, Suazo's austerity measures increased discontent among the Liberal Party's urban middle-class base who felt the effects of tax increases on consumer goods and import restrictions. Second, Suazo's handouts to his closest political supporters (irrespective of their economic needs) angered many businessmen and as a result, a powerful San Pedro Sula group around *La Prensa* and *El Heraldo* deserted the government. Third, and most important, as the November 1985 elections approached, Suazo's Liberal opponents realised that the president and his closest cabinet advisers were attempting to engineer an extension of Suazo's presidency (apparently inspired by a fortune-teller's prediction that he would rule for another four years). When that was blocked by the military and the US, the *suazocordovistas* switched their attention to trying to ensure that their choice for Suazo's successor, Oscar Mejía Arellano won the Liberal Party's nomination.

With their own presidential ambitons threatened, two Liberal leaders, the centre-right technocrat José Azcona del Hoyo and rural *caudillo* and president of Congress, Efraín Bú Girón, deserted the Suazo Córdova camp and began organising independently. They combined with the two other Liberal dissident factions (ALIPO divided into the Social Democrat MOLIDER and ALIPO in 1984) and the other opposition parties to demand publicly supervised primary elections within each party. Their problem was that they did not have the necessary two-thirds majority in Congress to overturn Suazo's personal veto over changes in the electoral law. So they targeted Suazo's control over the National Electoral Tribunal (TNE), which had enabled him to manipulate the reselection process in both the National and Liberal parties.

113

The TNE was especially important as it had the power to oversee nominations and electoral procedures. But of the five members of the TNE, a majority of three were loyal to Suazo, including the representative of the Supreme Court. At the end of March, Bú Girón rallied a 50-29 majority within Congress to fire the president of the Supreme Court and four other *suazocordovista* judges on minor charges of corruption (not for their systematic failure to comply with *habeas corpus* or to investigate disappearances), and replace them with judges not allied to Suazo. Smelling a 'technical *coup d'état'*, Suazo refused to recognise the Congressional action, ordered the five new judges arrested, and dispatched the *cobras* to block off the National Congress and Supreme Court buildings. Honduras had entered what *Tiempo* described as 'the most profound crisis of Honduran political life for the last 50 years'.

A political stalemate ensured for the next few weeks. A compromise solution was only reached on 20 May, following the intervention of the armed forces — who threatened to replace Suazo, the trade unions — who threatened a general strike, and the United States — who threatened to cut off aid if there was any rupture in the democratic image of the country. The Congressional nominee to the presidency of the Supreme Court was released, four members of the Supreme Court (except the president) were replaced, and the five new judges were

---

Presidential Candidates for 24 November Elections

Liberal Party

1) José Azcona Hoyo (*azconistas* and ALIPO)
2) Oscar Mejía Arellano *(suavocordovistas)*
3) Efraín Bú Girón *(bugistas)*
4) Carlos Roberto Reina (MOLIDER)

National Party

1) Juan Pablo Urrutia (Movement for Unity and Change)
2) Rafael Leonardo Callejas *(callejistas)*
3) Fernando Lardizábal Gilbert

PINU

1) Enrique Aguilar Cerrato

Christian Democrat Party

1) Hernán Corrales Padilla

---

asked to resign. No party was allowed to field an official candidate for the presidential elections, but all the various factions within each party were permitted to put up their own candidates on the day of the elections for the presidency, Congress and the municipalities. Totals, however, were to be by party with, for example, the Liberal presidential candidate who won the most votes taking the votes of the other Liberal candidates. The result was further fragmentation of the political parties. In the months that followed the constitutional crisis, as many as five candidates from the Liberal Party and five from the National Party were discussed as possible contenders in the 24 November presidential elections. By midnight on 24 September, a total of nine candidates had registered — four from the Liberal Party, three from the National Party and one each from PINU and the Christian Democrat Party (see box opposite).

It was not clear how much the compromise solution was a triumph for Suazo. Even though he could not now repeat his 1980 trick of rigging the Liberal Party primaries to ensure his candidature, as president he still maintained control over such institutions as the National Civil Registry (which plays a key role in deciding whether Honduran citizens have the necessary credentials to vote), and wielded considerable influence within the TNE.

On the surface, the constitutional crisis looked like a conflict between the executive and legislative branches of government. But in essence, the dispute went no deeper than feuding between the party bosses of the Liberal political machine. On the one hand, Suazo and his clique were struggling to maintain control over the government apparatus by means of fraud, corruption and manipulation of the electoral process. On the other, the 'reformers' were demanding internal party elections merely in an attempt to outwit Suazo and open up the political process to broader (i.e. their own) participation. But this squabbling over the eventual spoils of office was nothing new. Honduras' main political parties had always been run as patronage machines by party godfathers who, once in office, plundered the state's coffers.

The constitutional crisis revealed the weakness of US plans for the country. The original proposal had been to preserve the formal elements of democracy — a civilian president, parties and elections — 'hung out like a red light to attract customers', while the military ensured a secure US base and made the important decisions (in consultation with the US embassy). But the US was content with the trappings of Honduran democracy and frightened by social and economic reforms which could have extended popular participation. The Honduran political system simply degenerated into its familiar venality and self-interest.

Business As Usual

Just as Alvarez's successors left intact the political structures they inherited, they also maintained the economic model. The long-term aim of the original economic plan had been to reduce the public spending deficit, boost exports and attract new foreign investment. Even using these economic criteria, by mid-1985 it was clear that the model had failed.

Public Spending

Between 1979 and 1981, the fiscal deficit had trebled from 262 million lempiras (US$131 million) to 874 million lempiras (US$437 million), in which most of the increase was due to paying off the debt acquired by companies financed through CONADI. The government response to this was to cut public spending and increase taxes, but by 1984 the deficit had reached 931 million lempiras. According to a May 1984 publication by the Honduran College of Economists, the failure to reduce the deficit was due to the continuing debt repayments through CONADI, capital flight, administrative corruption in state projects, tax evasion, administrative deficiency in the collection of revenue, and excessive increases in military expenditure.

Taxes were increased on at least three occasions. Since rates of direct taxation on income are traditionally low in Honduras, the increases were therefore on sales and consumer taxes, which especially affected the middle classes and the urban poor. Foreign companies were not touched by the new taxation laws, although it has been calculated that an estimated US$25 million could be raised from an increase in the tax on banana exports to one dollar a box.

The government cut subsidies on a range of basic goods. Only five of an original 47 subsidies remained in force by May 1985. Spending on public health, education, agrarian reform and road construction was reduced, while the budget for defence and public security was increased. For example, in the 1985 budget, health and education spending represented less than 7 per cent of the national budget, while military spending consumed more than 30 per cent. In 1984 the Ministry of Health reported that of the 362 health centres in rural Honduras, 210 were shut down for lack of medicines, equipment or personnel. In contrast, the bill for Honduras' contribution to the construction of various military installations used in the joint manoeuvres came to more than US$25 million.

Despite Suazo's promises of 'a revolution in work and honesty', his administration was notorious for the inefiency and corruption of its public servants. In July 1983, a gift of 200 tons of powdered milk from the EEC (worth approximately US$200,000) disappeared; a number of bags later turned up in the markets of Tegucigalpa and San Pedro Sula. In February 1984, 37 tons of fertilisers also sent by the EEC to the peasant cooperative movement, FECORAH, were sold to private companies through the state-owned bank BANDESA. The government also had to continue to bail out companies originally funded by CONADI. In March 1984, the cement company Cementos de Honduras, owned by Faiz and Feizal Sikaffy, was nationalised after the brothers had run off to Miami with the CONADI-donated funds.

Balance of Payments

Imports were restricted by a 10 per cent across-the-board duty imposed back in 1981 and by 1985 had been reduced to some 70 per cent of 1979 levels. Industry and commerce were especially badly hit by the reduction in imports. Nearly one hundred small and medium-sized businesses went bankrupt between 1982 and 1983, and by 1984 industry was operating at 49 per cent of its capacity.

Exports failed to respond to a range of stimuli. Under the US administration's Caribbean Basin Initiative (CBI), a number of incentives were created to boost non-traditional exports such as citrus fruits, spring vegetables and some manufactured goods. But over 50 per cent of Honduras' export income continued to come from its two staple export crops, bananas and coffee. In the period 1981-83, Honduran exports diminished by an annual average of 5 per cent. The world market was saturated and consequently prices were low (for bananas), or export quotas tight (for coffee), leaving little room for expansion. Honduras' reserves were virtually exhausted and a continual shortage of dollars led to de facto import restrictions and intense competition for foreign exchange. In addition, by 1984 the national debt had risen to over US$2 billion.

Investment

The original Facussé memorandum had demanded incentives to both private and domestic investment. In the period 1977-80, private investment had almost doubled, from 445 million lempiras to 758 million. But by 1983, the figure had dropped back to 450 million, almost equal to the 1977 figure. Between 1980 and 1983 public investment, on the other hand, continued to increase from 410 million to 488 million. Foreign investment declined as a result of fears about the general crisis in the region, while opportunities for national capital were severely restricted by the general contraction of the Honduran economy.

Other economic indicators only serve to endorse the image of an economy in ruins: GNP per capita contracted by 12 per cent from 1980 to 1983, per capita income falling from 623 lempiras to 560 lempiras, lower than the 1977 figure. The reduction in average incomes could hardly have helped the 57 per cent of the population who in 1980 did not have an income sufficient to cover minimum food requirements. According to the planning ministry CONSUPLANE, open unemployment affected 21 per cent of the work force in 1984, three times its 1972 level. Fifty-seven per cent of those in work were underemployed. In all, a total of 43 per cent of the work force was affected by under- or unemployment.

President Suazo publicly admitted that the economic strategy was not working, but his administration's only remedy was to ask for more aid and more preferential treatment from the United States. But the Reagan administration was slow to increase its economic assistance to the Suazo government. Honduras' strategic value remained the priority for the Reagan administration, and not its desperate poverty. 'In Honduras today,' as one journalist wrote, 'it is much easier to find well-armed mercenaries in shiny boots than Honduran children with shoes'.

The Opposition

The present economic and political model is unable to meet the needs of the majority of Hondurans, but the opposition is too weak and divided to present a viable alternative.

The Honduran labour and peasant unions are well-organised, but deeply divided. The majority of workers and peasants pursue economic improvements through their unions and are at times prepared to take part in strike action or land seizures, but still vote for the traditional Liberal and National parties at elections. The reasons for this are diverse. First, family and local ties to the two parties remain strong. Second, there are constraints on union organisation. Despite the large numbers of union members, labour legislation stipulates that unions can only be formed in workplaces with over 25 employees, which inhibits trade union activity in much of the manufacturing sector, where small companies predominate. As a result, the unions often see their role as defending their economic and sectional advantages. On the northern coast, some 10,000 banana workers have a long tradition of labour militancy, but they are isolated from the rest of the country. In the urban economy, large numbers of street vendors and service sector workers, the 'underemployed', remain largely unorganised and form a reservoir of 'clients' for the political bosses in the traditional parties.

The peasant movement in particular has suffered from sectarianism, corruption and personal rivalries between leaders. In mid-1985 there were four main peasant federations and at least fifteen different peasant organisations. During the 1970s, the corruption of some peasant leaders led rival leaders to withdraw their supporters and form new organisations. Labour and peasant unions issued joint statements against Suazo's manoeuvrings during the constitutional crisis of April 1985, and led May Day demonstrations of more than 100,000 workers. But despite the appearance of unity, the movement remained divided along ideological grounds. The May Day demonstrations witnessed one march organised by the more left-wing United Federation of Workers (FUTH) and a second march organised jointly by the CGT and CTH. In addition, in late 1984, the UNC withdrew from the National Unity Front of Honduran Peasants (FUNACAMH), leaving the majority of the remaining organisations to form the National Congress of Rural Workers (CNTC) in early 1985, while the APROH-supported faction of ANACH split to form the Authentic National Congress of Honduran Peasants (CENACH).

While Alvarez remained in power, peasant organisations, and particularly the UNC, were severely restricted by the National Security legislation that defined land seizures as subversive acts. However, from 10-12 April 1985, the UNC coordinated over 60 peasant groups in the first national land seizure in ten years, which resulted in the arrest of around 140 peasant leaders. UNC leaders met with General Walter López within three days, and most of those arrested were soon released. The land invasions reflected the depth of peasant dissatisfaction with the slow pace of the agrarian reform under the Suazo administration, but there was little indication that it was a prelude to more radical political confrontation with the government.

The largest trade union and peasant federations are still dominated by the US labour organisations and advisers. The possibility of gaining limited improvements through union activity has preserved the appeal of reforming tendencies within the popular movement at the expense of more radical currents. The pro-Moscow (PCH) and pro-Peking (PCH-ML) Communist parties have preserved some influence. Much criticised for their 'top-down' methods, they nevertheless dominate the smaller union federations such as the FUTH and the CNTC, and the two teachers' unions, COLPROSUMAH and COPEMH. Members of both of these have taken repeated strike action over a range of economic issues. A six-week strike in 1982 was the toughest union challenge to the Suazo administration and led to the occupation of COLPROSUMAH's offices by government troops and the imposition of a new and compliant leadership.

In the late 1950s Communists had been influential in the formation of Honduras' first peasant union, FENACH. But following FENACH's destruction in 1963, the party opted to work with the working class, an approach more in accordance with Communist Party traditions. In the absence of a strong Communist presence, radical church activists became the main force behind the more progressive peasant federations of ACASCH and then the UNC in the 1960s and '70s. They also played a major role in the formation of the Christian Democrat Party (PDCH) in 1968. Differences within the UNC and the PDCH surfaced after the 1975 Los Horcones massacre. The right wing tacitly supported a tactical retreat, but the more radical wing favoured further mobilisation aimed at extending the agrarian reform. The divisions subsequently led in the late 1970s to the formation of a more combative peasant union, the National Union of Honduran Authentic Peasants (UNCAH), and the Socialist Party (PASOH), as splits from the UNC and the PDCH respectively.

A number of small and divided guerrilla groups emerged after the triumph of the Sandinistas in 1979, but they have failed to win significant popular support and have little influence in the major union organisations. The success of the Nicaraguan revolution and the failure of the left-wing alliance, the Honduran Patriotic Front (FPH), in the 1981 elections (when the FPH suffered constant harassment and failed to win a single seat) encouraged members of the communist parties, left-wing Christians and younger groups of radicalised students to make clandestine preparations for the armed struggle. The PCH-ML gave birth to the Morazanista Liberation Front (FMLNH); PASOH, the Socialist Party, linked up with the Central American Workers' Revolutionary Party (PRTC); and two other guerrilla organisations emerged among students at the National Autonomous University (UNAH): the Patriotic Revolutionary Forces (FPR) and the Cinchoneros Popular Liberation Movement (MPL).

These groups have enjoyed little success. The two most spectacular guerrilla actions organised by the Cinchoneros in 1982 ended without their main demands being met. Although the PRTC, FPR, Cinchoneros, FMLNH and PCH signed a document of unity in June 1983, there is little evidence that this has been implemented in practice. A guerrilla front launched by the PRTC in July 1983 ended in tragic failure. The PRTC had done little preparatory political work when they dispatched a guerrilla column from Nicaragua into the department of Olancho, and the group failed to make any effective contact with the local population. They were betrayed by two recruits and subsequently annihilated by the armed forces working with US advisers.

The destruction of a number of guerrilla safe houses in 1982-83 compounded the setbacks, and forced the orthodox Marxist parties to make a hasty re-evaluation of their earlier commitments to the armed struggle. During 1984 and 1985 the two Communist parties were able to recover lost ground by rebuilding bases within the FUTH and the teachers' movement. At the same time, the virtual elimination of PASOH following the Olancho debacle opened up space for the communists within the left-wing peasant organisation, UNCAH, where the party is again the dominant force.

Other sources of opposition have emerged in the 1980s, including the church. Honduran bishops have the reputation of adopting a low political profile and a more modest social role than some of their counterparts in El Salvador and Nicaragua. The development of grassroots Christian communities in the 1960s led to a slow radicalisation of the church's position. In the early 1970s certain sectors of the clergy began to speak out for the first time against the traditional power sectors of Honduran society, but after the Los Horcones massacre in 1975 the church adopted a more cautious stance. Early in 1980, the work of radical priests at the grassroots and particularly the protests of the diocese of Santa Rosa de Copán against Honduran participation in the massacre of Salvadorean refugees at the Sumpul river influenced the church to challenge the status quo again. In the pastoral letter of October 1982, 'On certain aspects of Honduran national reality', the bishops spoke out against corruption and human rights violations and in favour of social justice and peace in the region. The church also gave its tacit backing to the work of the two human rights committees, CODEH and COFADEH, and openly criticised government links with the Moonies' fund-raising body, CAUSA. More recently, *Inforpress* of 29 August 1985 reported that the archbishop of Tegucigalpa, Héctor Enrique Santos, had stated in reference to a possible war with Nicaragua that 'Honduras must be independent, and must not be manipulated by any power', which many interpreted as a clear confirmation of the church's opposition to a war with Nicaragua and the presence of US troops in the country.

The principal threat to the domination of the Liberal and National parties comes not from any electoral opposition but from their own internal fragmentation. According to a report of the Honduran Institute for Socio-economic Research (INSEH), at the beginning of 1985 there were eleven different factions within the National Party, and five within the Liberal Party. Most of these factions, and the various presidential candidates from the traditional parties, continued to reflect personal disputes over the control of the parties, and not differences over policy. Dissatisfaction with the corruption and economic incompetence of the Suazo government has been translated

121

into some support for both the ALIPO and MOLIDER tendencies of the Liberal Party and the group around the former public works minister, José Azcona del Hoyo. But none of the factions can rely on organised support from the grassroots. MOLIDER, PINU and the PDCH are opposed to the presence of US troops in the country and in favour of Honduran neutrality and social reform, and all of them are likely to benefit from the increase in the number of deputies in Congress to 132 (50 more than in the 1981 elections). But with no party or coalition representing major organised popular forces, and with the Reagan administration firmly entrenched in the White House, the people of Honduras can hope for little improvement from the elections in November 1985.

Appendices

Appendix 1(a). Joint US-Honduran Manoeuvres 1981-1985 (land based)

Note: Major US-Honduras manoeuvres are in bold type, to distinguish them from smaller-scale or counterinsurgency operations.

Name	Date	Activities and Location	Participants
Falcon's Eye	Oct. 1981	Naval and landing manoeuvres near Puerto Cortés, Honduras.	300 troops, including 130 US personnel; 6 ships.
Combined Movement	26 July-5 Aug. 1982	Construction of permanent Honduran base at Durzuna, 25 miles from the Nicaraguan border.	30 US support troops, US supplied C-130 transport planes, Huey and Chinook helicopters.
Big Pine I (Ahuas Tara I)	2 Feb.-6 Feb. 1983	Mock defence of Honduras from attack by 'Red Army', 25 miles from the Nicaraguan border.	1,600 US army, navy, and air force personnel; 4,000 Honduran troops.
Big Pine II	6 Aug. 1983-8 Feb. 1984	Field training exercises including weapons and counterinsurgency training and tactics to repel artillery and tank attacks; also practice bombing runs at San Lorenzo, massive amphibious landing near Puerto Castilla; field training exercise in eastern Honduras, near the Nicaraguan border.	5,500 US army, navy and air force troops, including combat troops and navy tactical air crews; two aircraft carriers with battle group escorts; several thousand Honduran troops.
Emergency Deployment Readiness	19-29 March 1984	'No notice' exercises involving tactics, medical, communication and survival capabilities, 25 miles north of Tegucigalpa.	40 US Special Forces and 150-200 Honduran Special Forces.
Kilo Punch	24-26 March 1984	Paratrooping near the Palmerola airfield and securing of the San Lorenzo airfield by combined airborne and air assault	350 US personnel and 130 Honduran airborne infrantrymen.

(Granadero I)	June 1984	...systems of airfield at Catacuagua and Jamastrán, near the Salvadorean and Nicaraguan borders respectively, in order to accommodate C-130 transport planes, counterinsurgency training, and helicopter assault operation.	...force personnel, and additional 750-800 US troops; 1,200 Honduran troops. Panamanian, Guatemalan and Salvadorean troops invited, of whom only the Salvadoreans accepted.
Lightning II	13 April 1984	Paratroop assault to secure an operations base from which to stage an attack on an airfield. Near Aguacate, 120 miles north-east of Tegucigalpa, and 60 miles from the Nicaraguan border.	170 Honduran Special Forces and 120 US army forces.
Operation Lempira I	23 July-6 Aug. 1984	Parachute jump near Palmerola and mock helicopter attack at Marcala.	Small team of US army Green Berets and troops from Honduran army's 10th Infantry Battalion.
Operation Lempira II	20-31 Aug. 1984	Practising counterinsurgency techniques in west and south-west of Comayagua department.	200 Green Berets and 3 battalions from Honduran army.
Crown Dragonfly	22-27 Sept. 1984	Bombing runs near San Pedro Sula and Palmerola air base.	4 US A-37 attack planes and 8 from Honduran air force.
Air Force Exercise	28 Oct.-17 Nov. 1984	Exercises near Palmerola, La Mesa and San Lorenzo.	A-37 planes from Pennsylvania Air National Guard, and observation planes from Howard Air Force Base, Panama.
Big Pine III	11 Feb.-3 May 1985	(i) Escorpión: simulated defence of Honduras from Nicaragua, 5kms from Nicaraguan border in Las Hormigas, Choluteca.	3,000 US (including units of US National Guard) and 5,000 Honduran troops, 20 Scorpion, 17 M-60 and 17 M-113, and 5 Russian tanks.
		(ii) Chicatic: counterinsurgency training in Yoro.	3,000 US and Honduran troops.
Universal Trek '85	12 April-5 May 1985	Amphibious landings with support of attack helicopters and various ships on north-eastern coast of Honduras.	7,000 US and 2,300 Honduran troops, 14 armoured trucks, 750 marines, 4 A-37 planes, 24 helicopters, guided missile cruiser, destroyer, and frigate.

Name	Date	Activities and Location	Participants
Cabañas '85	7 June-27 Sept. 1985	(i) 7 June-11 Sept.: engineering works, including road construction in Yoro.	US engineers and Honduran 1st Infantry Battalion.
		(ii) 5-10 July: heavy artillery exercises in Santa Barbara.	2nd Artillery Battalion from Fort Ord, California and 600 Honduran troops.
		(iii) 26 Aug.-27 Sept.: counterinsurgency training in Yoro.	1,800 troops.

Sources: Central American Historical Institute, Washington; *Inforpress*; NARMIC, Pennsylvania.

Appendix 1(b). US Naval Manoevures off the Coast of Honduras and Nicaragua

Name	Date	Activities and Location	Participants
Readex-82, Ocean Venture	April 1982	Naval exercises in the Caribbean.	Various US ships.
Naval manoeuvres	July 1983	Exercises involving two naval task forces off the Pacific and Atlantic coasts, to practise possible blockade of Nicaragua.	Aircraft carrier *Ranger* and 7 ships on the Pacific coast (later joined by battleship *New Jersey* and 6 other ships), aircraft carrier *Coral Sea* and battle group of 5 ships on Atlantic coast.
Ocean Venture	20 April– 6 May 1984	Naval exercise in the Caribbean sea, Florida straits, Gulf of Mexico and the Atlantic Ocean. Involved the evacuation of 300 people from the US base at Guantánamo Bay, Cuba, live-fire training and mock bombing runs.	30,000 personnel from all branches of the US military; aircraft carrier *America* and 350 support ships.
King's Guard	26 April– 7 May 1984	Coastal surveillance exercise in Gulf of Fonseca, to practise interception techniques.	500 US, 75 Honduran and 100 Salvadorean personnel, 2 US destroyers and patrol boats.
King's Guard	8-19 Nov. 1984	Coastal surveillance in Gulf of Fonseca.	One US ship, several hundred US, Honduran and Salvadorean troops.

Sources: Central American Historical Institute and NARMIC.

Appendix 2. Subsidiaries of United Brands (United Fruit) and Castle and Cooke (Standard Fruit) in Honduras

United Brands
United Fruit Company

Agriculture
Fábrica de Aceites de Palma
Productos Acuáticos Terrestres (PATSA)
Tela Railroad: fruit production, cattle production

Food processing
Compañía Agrícola de Río Tinto
Frigorífica Hondureña
Numar de Honduras: vegetable oil processing
Unimar: palm oil

Industry
Caribbean Enterprises
Empresa Hondureña de Vapores
Fábrica de Cajas de Cartón
Polymer: rubber and plastics
Servicio de Investigación Agrícola Tropical (SIATSA)
TRT Telecommunications
(United Fruit products are often marketed under the brand name 'Chiquita')

Castle and Cooke
Standard Fruit Company

Agriculture
Compañía Bananera Antillana
Dole Pineapple of Honduras
Semillas Mejoradas
Servicios Agrícolas
Standard Fruit and Steamship

Food Processing
Cervecería Hondureña: beer and soft drinks (four branches)
Cervecería Tegucigalpa
Compañía Agrícola Industrial Ceibeña: vegetable oil processing
Enlatadora del Campo
Frutera Hondureña
Industria Aceitera Hondureña: cotton seed oil processing

Industry/Finance
Aceros Industriales
Banco del Comercio
Envases Industriales de Honduras: metal container manufacturing
Fábrica de Manteca y Jabón Atlántida: oil, margarine and soap
Manufacturera de Cartón: paper box manufacturing

Nacional Inmobiliaria
Plásticos: plastic material manufacturing
Servicios de Investigaciones Aéreas

Source: Tom Barry et al., *Dollars and Dictators,* Zed Press, 1983.

Appendix 3. Salvadorean Refugees in Honduras

Salvadorean refugees have been crossing into Honduras in large numbers since 1980. By late 1985, there were around 20,000 of them, the vast majority settled in three camps — Colomoncagua, San Antonio, and Mesa Grande (see map, p.89) — along the border with Morazán, under the protection of the United Nations High Commission for Refugees (UNHCR).

Since Honduras is not a signatory to the 1951 and 1967 Geneva accords on refugees, UNHCR's position in the country is not wholly secure, and the Honduran authorities have considerable influence over the treatment of the refugees and the conditions of their stay in Honduras. CONARE, the National Refugee Commission, was created in 1980 to manage the rapidly growing refugee population. Headed by retired army Colonel Abraham Turcios, it puts the camps effectively under the jurisdiction of the Honduran military.

Unlike the Nicaraguan Miskitos, the Salvadorean refugees have always been regarded with suspicion and hostility by the Honduran authorities. They have shown a very high degree of community organisation, practical activity and determination unsettling to their hosts. Both the Honduran and Salvadorean armies have long claimed that the camps, particularly Colomoncagua and San Antonio, are sanctuaries for Salvadorean guerrillas — a view echoed by the US, to whom their presence is an embarrassing obstacle to the joint military manoeuvres. That the US sees the Salvadorean refugees as a counter-insurgency problem is clear from the State Department's February 1985 'Non-policy paper' on Colomoncagua, which suggests that closing down Colomoncagua camp would render the border area more secure and make it 'easier for the Honduran military to make sweeps of the area and to disrupt any regional insurgency activity there'.

In fact, the refugees have been under constant pressure to leave the border ever since 1981. Mesa Grande, the largest and most overcrowded camp, and the furthest from the border, is itself a product of the first big upheaval, when some 3,000 refugees were forcibly removed from the area of La Virtud. That operation took six months (Nov. 1981-April 1982) and during it 34 refugees and four workers from the international relief agency CARITAS were killed and 45 Hondurans and Salvadoreans disappeared. Almost immediately UNHCR began talking of a fresh relocation of the 8,000 refugees in Colomoncagua and San Antonio camps, plus the 500 Guatemalans in El Tesoro, to a series of possible sites, finally deciding on Olanchito, several hundred miles away in the department of Yoro. UNHCR argued that the refugees would thus have more land and would become more independent of international aid, and also that they would be safer away from the border. The refugees, international agency workers in the camps, and human rights organisations disagreed, considering that the real motive was to militarise the border and close it to the entry of more Salvadoreans. They resolutely opposed the move.

Throughout 1984 and into 1985, the pressures for relocation mounted. From mid-1984 repatriation to El Salvador was increasingly put forward as an option. This was even less acceptable to the refugees than relocation, and was a clear breach of the January 1981 agreement between the Honduran government and UNHCR, which stipulated that Honduras would repatriate the refugees only if conditions in El Salvador permitted their safe return, and then not against the wishes of the refugees. Since then, the pressure on the refugees has increased as bombing raids over Morazán came nearer, surveillance aircraft overflew the camps, international workers were harassed and sacked, and Honduran military patrols in and around the camps grew larger and more aggressive. By August 1985, counterinsurgency troops were permanently stationed around Colomoncagua and San Antonio and an estimated 800 Honduran soldiers were guarding the frontier, only a few kilometres away, discouraging more refugees from crossing. On 29 August 1985 several hundred Honduran soldiers burst into Colomoncagua camp shooting indiscriminately, ostensibly seeking guerrillas, and killed two people (one a two-month-old baby), wounded up to 50 more, and flew ten prisoners off in a helicopter. Early in September, the Honduran minister of the interior announced in a letter to UNHCR representatives in Tegucigalpa that the refugees in Colomoncagua and San Antonio would be relocated to the already overcrowded Mesa Grande camp. UNHCR took a more supportive line towards the refugees than previously, but it still held back from refusing relocation point-blank.

The long-standing border dispute between Honduras and El Salvador has not prevented the two governments from collaborating on several occasions in military actions along the border. On 10-11 July 1985, Presidents Duarte and Suazo issued a joint communiqué expressing the support of both governments for repatriation on the grounds that the democratic process in El Salvador had created conditions suitable for the refugees' return. However, since the Duarte government took office in June 1984 civilians have continued to bear the brunt of the Salvadorean civil war. As Salvadorean army counterinsurgency operations have increasingly concentrated on clearing the guerrilla-controlled zones of Chalatenango and Morazán, there has been no let-up in the number of refugees flowing into Honduras.

Mandy Macdonald

Further Reading

Juan Arancibia, *Honduras: un estado nacional?,* Ediciones Guaymuras, Tegucigalpa, 1984.

Father J. Guadalupe Carney, *To be a Revolutionary,* Harper and Row, 1984.

William H. Durham, *Scarcity and Survival in Central America: Ecological Origins of the Soccer War,* Stanford University Press, 1979.

Víctor Meza, *Historia del movimiento obrero hondureño,* Ediciones Guaymuras, Tegucigalpa, 1980.

James A. Morris, *Honduras: Caudillo Politics and Military Rulers,* Westview Press, 1984.

Mario Posas, *El Movimiento campesino hondureño,* Ediciones Guaymuras, Tegucigalpa, 1981.

Mario Posas and Rafael del Cid, *La construcción del sector público y del estado nacional en Honduras,* EDUCA, San José, Costa Rica, 1981.

Mark B. Rosenberg, Honduran Scorecard: Military and Democrats in Central America, *Caribbean Review,* January 1983.

Steven Volk, *Honduras: On the Border of War,* NACLA report, Nov.-Dec. 1981.

Periodicals

Boletín Informativo, Centro de Documentación de Honduras (CEDOH), Apartado Postal 1882, Tegucigalpa.

Honduras Briefing, Central America Information Service, 1 Amwell Street, London EC1R 1UL.

Honduras Update, Honduras Information Centre, 1 Summer Street, Somerville, Massachusetts 02143, USA.